LOVE
Calling

Enjoy :) -

Mikaela Kate

ISBN: 9780578408514

Book Formatting & E-book Design by Amit Dey | amitdey2528@gmail.com

Book Cover Design & Interior Design by Briana Pettit | bpettit3.30@gmail.com

Dedication

The early years of a child's life are pivotal in helping cultivate a true understanding of love, and the power it holds which is why I am dedicating this book to my grandmothers. Grandma Ruth and Grandma Gretchen played a very important role in my childhood. Growing up I remember endless games of hide and go seek, checkers, and Bingo, as well as eating the best apple pie you'll ever taste and fun shopping adventures. Each in their own way, they poured out love to me.

Attending all my school activities, they were faithfully my biggest fans in the stands. Whether it was basketball or softball game or a musical concert, they showed up early (even before the janitor) and I saw their smiling faces from the first-row bleacher looking at me with incredible delight.

As a child these are the instances you can often take for granted, and only now as I reflect, do I see how crucial this foundation of love was for me. Years later that love continued to open wide my own journey of knowing the heart and love of my Father in Heaven which in turn gave me the courage and confidence to write these words so boldly.

From my earliest of days God, Love Himself, was calling on me time and time again. I pray His words will speak His love to you as well.

Table of Contents

Introduction

They say a picture is worth a 1,000 words, and although that might be true there is still incredible power in the written word.

A great book, a sentimental letter, or a riveting novel all have their purpose, place and power.

Thanks to my parents I have always had a love for books, a love they instilled in me at a very young age. In just one sentence you can find yourself connecting with the characters as if they are sitting next to you.

In high school I remember lying in bed one night as I was reading the book, *The 7 Habits of Highly Effective People* by Stephen Covey and in that moment thought, "I could do this. I could write books."

Years went by and eventually that passing thought became a reality. As a naïve teenager I didn't realize how hard the process would be, but slow and steady as the pen hit the paper this book came to life.

My desire is that these words would pierce your heart as they have pierced mine, and it would feel as if Love Himself is sitting next to you. I pray you would read them knowing they are from the Father's heart meant just for you…because they are.

May they change you, inspire you, and cause you to love life all the more – just as they have for me.

With Love,
Mikaela Kate

January
Devotional

Say Goodbye and Say Hello!

Proper goodbyes and proper hellos are crucial to each new season. To fully say goodbye to what was and all the joy and pain, which accompanied that time is a critical piece of the journey. Don't be so quick to rush into the new season and forget to fully close the last chapter. Take time to say a proper goodbye, give a fitting farewell and be thankful for who and what was in that season. Then you'll be able to step forward ready to write a new chapter and say hello to what's ahead!

Psalm 86:11

¹¹ *Teach me your way, LORD,*
that I may rely on your faithfulness;
give me an undivided heart,
that I may fear your name.

It's All About Position!

Position yourself for training, growth, and expansion. My eyes are on the earth looking for individuals who are ready to run, ready to push through the mud and keep their eyes on the prize. Posture your mind to keep learning and digesting information as it comes to you. As you move about the day, I'll add to your life, giving you what you need to know and connecting you with the right individuals. Keep your mind open, honest, and humble and watch how I'll advance you. This is your time, this is your season – get ready to run!

_____

_____

_____

_____

_____

_____

_____

Psalm 18:34-36

[34] He trains my hands for battle;
my arms can bend a bow of bronze.
[35] You make your saving help my shield,
and your right hand sustains me;
your help has made me great.
[36] You provide a broad path for my feet,
so that my ankles do not give way.

Every. Single. Day.

Every day I am moving towards you and I am looking to accelerate your journey. Every day I look for opportunities to bump into you and give you a nudge and a wink. Every day I seek you in hopes that you will find me. Every day I have you on my mind, on my heart and I am longing to speak to. Every day and every moment you are the one I have my eye on. Every day I am pursuing you and looking to accelerate and ignite your passion and purposes. Every day I desire to bless you. Every day you can count on each of these things. Every. Single. Day.

_____

_____

_____

_____

_____

_____

_____

_____

_____

_____

Psalm 55:22

22 Cast your cares on the LORD
and he will sustain you;
he will never let
the righteous be shaken.

You're Right on Track.

It may seem like you're lost, like you don't know where you're going, floundering without a purpose or plan. The road may seem incredibly bumpy, and the destination might seem like it's completely out of sight, but my charge to you today is to keep going with one foot in front of the other. Keep walking, with your eyes ahead. Don't hesitate and I will bless your efforts and magnify your voice. Life may seem more like a tornado filled with chaos, but I see your true reality and you're right on track.

_____

_____

_____

_____

_____

Isaiah 43:1-2

¹ But now, this is what the LORD SAYS—
he who created you, Jacob,
he who formed you, Israel:
"Do not fear, for I have redeemed you;
I have summoned you by name; you are mine.
² When you pass through the waters,
I will be with you;
and when you pass through the rivers,
they will not sweep over you.
When you walk through the fire,
you will not be burned;
the flames will not set you ablaze.

6

You are that Warrior!

I've made you like a warrior - fast, nimble, and able to adjust with great flexibility. You are fierce, strong, and always being prepared for the battle ahead. You have everything you need and are surrounded by an army ready to help you. Turn your ears to me, Your Commander. I will give the charge. I will sound the horn, and you'll know when it's your time to GO. I am strategically calling the shots from above, and you will not be defeated. You will see your reward, and you'll look back and see my hand masterfully giving you the victory. You are a warrior, full of courage, strength and much perseverance. Take charge today!

_____

_____

_____

_____

_____

_____

_____

_____

_____

Jeremiah 1:5

[5] *"Before I formed you in the womb I knew[a] you,*
before you were born I set you apart;
I appointed you as a prophet to the nations."

Go for It!

Go for it. I know you're a timid, scared and maybe even completely frightened at moving forward, but I am here. I am with you, and it's my voice you're following. Trust that I see beyond your immediate situation, and I am pushing you out beyond the waters and setting your course further than you could ever imagine. I am proud of you, so incredibly proud of your efforts. However small they may seem to you, they equate to leaps and bounds in my Kingdom. So, go for it today, take that step of faith because I am right here with you!

_____

_____

_____

_____

_____

_____

_____

_____

_____

_____

1 Peter 5:8-9

[8] *Be alert and of sober mind. Your enemy the devil prowls around like a roaring lion looking for someone to devour.* [9] *Resist him, standing firm in the faith, because you know that the family of believers throughout the world is undergoing the same kind of sufferings.*

Perfectly Connected

You are perfectly connected to every ounce of who I am. This is my desire all throughout the day – to meet you again and again and speak clearly to you so that understanding and wisdom continues to flow through your heart and mind. Connection points are what I am seeking, true moments where I hear your heart and you hear mine. This is where life flows, love awakens, and you begin to get clarity. Let me connect with you today, in a new and fresh way and watch how I'll show up!

_____
_____
_____
_____
_____
_____
_____
_____
_____
_____
_____
_____

Matthew 14:28

²⁸ "Lord, if it's you," Peter replied,
"tell me to come to you on the water."

Ask, Seek & Knock.

Before you rush into work, before you begin your tasks for the day, before you have that first meeting, sit with me awhile. Talk with me and hear my heart. I want to give you secrets. I want to give you clarity. I want to give you inspiration. For I know what you need before you even have need for it. Ask, seek, and knock before you start your day and see how I might answer. See how I might respond, and trust me that this moment of "pause" will give you what you need.

_____

_____

_____

_____

_____

_____

_____

_____

_____

_____

_____

Luke 11:9-10
[9] "So I say to you: Ask and it will be given to you;
seek and you will find; knock and the door will be opened to you.
[10] For everyone who asks receives; the one who seeks finds;
and to the one who knocks, the door will be opened.

Go Low to Go High

Showing them whose boss, giving them a taste of their own medicine – pure revenge. That's not who you are. That's not who I've created you to be. You carry love, honor, respect and dignity. You walk with integrity and seek to bring reconciliation. You don't give someone what they "deserve", but you pour out grace, acceptance, and unconditional love again and again. This is who you are and who I've created you to be. You don't keep the world's standard, instead lower yourself understanding that in doing so you rise above.

_____

_____

_____

_____

_____

_____

_____

_____

_____

_____

James 1:19-20

[19] My dear brothers and sisters, take note of this:
Everyone should be quick to listen, slow to speak
and slow to become angry; [20] because human anger does
not produce the righteousness that God desires.

Nothing is Holding You Back.

Nothing is holding you back. Nothing is standing in your way. No one or no thing can stop the momentum which I am building in your life. I am creating a path for you. I am moving mountains, splitting rivers, and making a way where it looks like there's no way. So, rush forward today, and push past the resistance, the torment, and the pain, and fight your way to the finish. Nothing is holding you back from getting to your destiny. Nothing is holding you back from receiving the full measure of my love, presence, and glory. What man intends for harm, I use for good, so watch as I usher you forward today.

_____

_____

_____

_____

_____

_____

_____

_____

_____

_____

Deuteronomy 8:1

⁸ *Be careful to follow every command I am giving you today, so that you may live and increase and may enter and possess the land the LORD PROMISED ON OATH TO YOUR ANCESTORS.*

You Are…Unstoppable!

You are confident, unstoppable and resilient in your pursuits. You have clear goals, and defined values you live by each and every day. You are learning to be your best friend, building yourself up and reaffirming who you are each and every day. You are filled with love and give out grace. You are accomplishing your goals and living your dreams. Each day you awake with energy, joy and determination. You are growing, changing, and expanding your influence. You are all these qualities and so much more! Preach it, speak it and believe it!

_____

_____

_____

_____

_____

_____

_____

_____

_____

_____

Psalm 23:6

⁶Surely your goodness and love will follow me
all the days of my life,
and I will dwell in the house of the LORD
forever.

13

See the Vision & Run!

Is something keeping you from moving ahead? Take an honest look at your life. What have I called you to in this season? Evaluate who or what is holding you back and keeping you from accomplishing all that I have for you. I am moving the Heavens for you and removing obstacles in your path. Be faithful, be diligent, and be consistent day in and day out with the opportunities in front of you. Each day I am building upon your life and growing you inside and out. No longer will doubt, fear or worry hold you back from your goals because nothing holds you back. Nothing.

_____

_____

_____

_____

_____

_____

_____

Mark 1:1-3

The beginning of the good news about Jesus the Messiah,[a] the Son of God,[b]2 as it is written in Isaiah the prophet:
"I will send my messenger ahead of you,
who will prepare your way"[c]
3 "a voice of one calling in the wilderness,
'Prepare the way for the Lord,
make straight paths for him.'"[d]

Tune Me in Today!

Give your body a detox today. Shut down the TV, turn off the phone and close the door. Hear my voice today without distractions, without the buzz of the world outside and truly dial into my words. There is so much I want to tell you, so much I desire to say. There's a calmness I want to bring, a peace within your soul that only I can give you. If only for a moment, shut out the other voices today and tune in again to my voice – the one that will pour out life to you today.

_____

_____

_____

_____

_____

_____

_____

_____

_____

_____

_____

Isaiah 30:21

21 Whether you turn to the right or to the left,
your ears will hear a voice behind you, saying,
"This is the way; walk in it."

You. Are. Ok.

Y ou're ok. It may seem like the world around you is controlling every piece of your life and you're spinning out of control, but this is not reality. I declare today that you are ok. Inside and outside I am taking care of you and providing your every need. You're ok. Your circumstances don't define you. They do not control your inner world and how you react. Take charge today and know that I see you, and I am holding you steady. You're ok. Actually, MORE than ok!

_____

_____

_____

_____

_____

_____

_____

_____

_____

_____

_____

_____

1 Peter 5:6-7

⁶ Humble yourselves, therefore, under God's mighty hand, that he may lift you up in due time. ⁷ Cast all your anxiety on him because he cares for you.

You Are Enough.

Every poster, billboard, commercial and advertisement screams at you, "You are not enough!" Be slimmer, trimmer, and more toned. Be smarter, sharper, and more educated. Be richer, quicker, and faster. From every angle you feel the pressure to do more and be more. Little does the world know that **you are enough**. Inside and outside you have everything you need, and who you are is enough. No more striving or performing to bend to the standards of the world. I've made you perfectly just as you are, so disregard the advertisements. Rest in the assurance that you are enough today.

_____

_____

_____

_____

_____

_____

_____

Psalm 23:1-3

¹ *The LORD IS MY SHEPHERD, I LACK NOTHING.*
² *He makes me lie down in green pastures,*
he leads me beside quiet waters,
³ *he refreshes my soul.*
He guides me along the right paths
for his name's sake.

The Tape in Your Head.

There's a tape that plays in your head. It goes on repeat again and again. It talks to you, speaks to you and directs you in the way you should go. Little do you realize that you control this tape. You command the words it plays and the sentences that fill your mind. You decide if the tape will be positive, negative, full of love or full of hate. This tape is written and produced by you, so choose wisely today the words you listen to for in them are the power of life and death.

_____

_____

_____

_____

_____

_____

_____

_____

_____

_____

_____

_____

Proverbs 4:4
⁴ Then he taught me, and he said to me,
"Take hold of my words with all your heart;
keep my commands, and you will live.

With Me...

With me you receive clarity, perspective and insight. With me you gain momentum, energy, and wisdom into the future. With me you move from feeling defeated to the position of overcomer. With me you gain confidence, self-esteem, and wisdom. With me you live with faith, hope and love. With me you gain courage, tenacity, and a sound mind. With me you operate in power and authority. With me you gain the strength, determination and resolve to keep going. The key in it all is to *remain with me*...and in doing so you will bear much fruit.

_____

_____

_____

_____

_____

_____

_____

John 15:5-8

[5] *"I am the vine; you are the branches. If you remain in me and I in you, you will bear much fruit; apart from me you can do nothing.* [6] *If you do not remain in me, you are like a branch that is thrown away and withers; such branches are picked up, thrown into the fire and burned.* [7] *If you remain in me and my words remain in you, ask whatever you wish, and it will be done for you.* [8] *This is to my Father's glory, that you bear much fruit, showing yourselves to be my disciples.*

19

Who's Around You Today?

Pay attention to the people I am putting around you. What are they like? How old are they? Where do they like to hang out? Notice the people I am drawing you toward, but also who are being drawn to you. We are connected by relationships. One person to another I create bonds, unity, and a force between you. This is where life takes place and where environments are transformed. Before you rush onto your day, mindlessly ticking off boxes, look at those who I've placed around you and make them your priority and keep them as your focus.

_____

_____

_____

_____

_____

_____

_____

_____

_____

_____

_____

_____

1 John 3:16

¹⁶ *This is how we know what love is: Jesus Christ laid down his life for us. And we ought to lay down our lives for our brothers and sisters.*

Stay Focused. Stay Diligent.

Stay diligent. Stay constant. Stay focused. Stay determined. There's no telling what's around the corner, what opportunities lie ahead and what moments of breakthrough are at your door step. It is time for you to advance, to stay sharp and steady on the tasks and people I've placed in front of you. Stay attentive. Stay intentional. Stay persistent and remain constant in your day-to-day activities. Then you'll be prepared and then you'll be ready when my voice says, "It is time!"

_____

_____

_____

_____

_____

_____

_____

_____

Ephesians 6:14-17

14 Stand firm then, with the belt of truth buckled around your waist, with the breastplate of righteousness in place, 15 and with your feet fitted with the readiness that comes from the gospel of peace. 16 In addition to all this, take up the shield of faith, with which you can extinguish all the flaming arrows of the evil one. 17 Take the helmet of salvation and the sword of the Spirit, which is the word of God.

A New Day Full of Possibilities.

Wake up my child for today is a new day, full of new possibilities. I don't go back and recount all the mistakes you think you made or the opportunities you think you missed. I only look ahead with eyes of faith, hope and love. This is my posture, so now let it be yours. Break off those rearview mirrors and lists in your head of what was and what should have been. That's not the list I read from nor should it be yours. Start fresh today and start a new, for my mercies are new every morning!

_____

_____

_____

_____

_____

_____

_____

_____

_____

_____

_____

Lamentations 3:22-23

²² *Because of the LORD'S GREAT LOVE WE ARE NOT CONSUMED,*
for his compassions never fail.
²³ *They are new every morning;*
great is your faithfulness.

Rise and Shine. Your Time is Now!

It is time my dear, time to rise and time to shine. No more holding back, no more resisting the change. It is time to stand up, make a name for yourself, and face the noise. It seems hard. It seems impossible. It seems like no one is for you, but these are the moments when I breakthrough, and your hard work pays off. Stand up tall today, walk with confidence, and declare boldly what you have to say. There's no stopping you, you're on your way – greater things are in store!

_____

_____

_____

_____

_____

_____

_____

_____

_____

_____

Psalm 18:32-33
32 It is God who arms me with strength
and keeps my way secure.
33 He makes my feet like the feet of a deer;
he causes me to stand on the heights.

You and Me and Me and You!

Y ou and I are a partnership. Where you go, I go. Where I go, you go. We are in this together. I know it can feel like you're all alone, drifting without a captain, but that couldn't be farther from the truth. We are a team, a force to be reckoned with, and a dynamic duo. Together we make things happen. Consult with me, pick my brain and we'll figure it out together. You and me and me and you. We're unstoppable and there's no telling how high or far we will go! TOGETHER we'll do great things!

_____

_____

_____

_____

_____

_____

_____

_____

_____

_____

_____

_____

Psalm 16:7

⁷ I will praise the LORD, WHO COUNSELS ME;
even at night my heart instructs me.

Check in with Me – I am Full of Answers.

Dial into my voice again and again and again. You may hear my whisper at the start of the day or at the end of the day when all is quiet, but even throughout the day I long to speak to you. Check in with me, ask me how I am doing, and where I am moving. I am an ever-present God full of answers, wisdom and insight. Take a step back, breathe again and dial into my heart. Here you'll find me and here I am waiting.

_____

_____

_____

_____

_____

_____

_____

_____

_____

_____

_____

Proverbs 24:14

*¹⁴ Know also that wisdom is like honey for you:
If you find it, there is a future hope for you,
and your hope will not be cut off.*

I See You, Always I See You.

I see you. I see your efforts and notice all you do for the good of those around you. You might not get the "thank you" or "good job" or pats on the back, but man's approval comes and goes but my affirmation is all that matters. Draw close to me today and let me tell you how proud I am of you, how thankful I am for all that you do, and how I observe every big and little thing you make time for. I see it all and could not be prouder to call you my child. I see you my friend, especially when you think no one else does. I do.

_____

_____

_____

_____

_____

_____

_____

_____

_____

_____

_____

Psalm 73:23-24

²³ *Yet I am always with you;*
you hold me by my right hand.
²⁴ *You guide me with your counsel,*
and afterward you will take me into glory.

26

Use Your Voice – Let's Hear It!

Worship me this day. Sing a new song to me. Use your voice to blast out your every thanksgiving, need and desire. It's in the praises where you come alive. It's the utterances of your voice where life starts to make sense. I am not promising all the answers will come rushing in, but clarity of your heart and mind will give you peace to walk out this day. Sometimes just the simplest of whispers allow your heart to move. So, declare something today. Say it out loud and watch how I move.

Psalm 100:4-5

⁴ *Enter his gates with thanksgiving*
and his courts with praise;
give thanks to him and praise his name.
⁵ *For the LORD IS GOOD AND HIS LOVE ENDURES FOREVER;*
his faithfulness continues through all generations.

For Good is the Enemy of Great.

The enemy wants you distracted by "good" things. Maybe helping out a neighbor, running errands for a friend, or serving on a committee. All good things, great things in fact, but keep your energy on me and listen to my agenda. Listen to my plans for you and keep in step in me. My steps are easy and my burdens are light. Keep your attention on me and say goodbye to those seemingly "good" distractions!

_____

_____

_____

_____

_____

_____

_____

_____

_____

_____

_____

Matthew 11:28-30

[28] *"Come to me, all you who are weary and burdened,*
and I will give you rest. [29] *Take my yoke upon you and learn from me,*
for I am gentle and humble in heart, and you will find rest for your
souls. [30] *For my yoke is easy and my burden is light."*

Come – Let Me Talk to You!

I want to talk to you - the one who I call special, chosen, and highly favored. This year is meant for the heights. There are no limits on you, no ceilings over your head, and barriers around you. When I say these words, I speak truth that my promises will come and will not return void. As I see YOU perfectly, I see that your name is written in the books where I have chosen you specifically. Let me remind you of those things, which are hidden in your heart, tucked away in your soul, and allow them to awaken you today.

_____

_____

_____

_____

_____

_____

_____

_____

_____

_____

Luke 10:20

[20] *However, do not rejoice that the spirits submit to you, but rejoice that your names are written in heaven."*

You're About to Take Off!

Y ou're about to take off. In fact, you are already on your way. This is the start of something great, something grand, something big. In fact, something has already begun. Tasks, appointments, and divine connections are being arranged and orchestrated as we speak. Your voice is being released and destiny is unfolding. You can't stop it or prevent it from happening, but your job is to only to rest in my presence, sit at my feet, and stand at attention to my voice. Get ready my dear, for your time has come and, in fact, it's already here!

Isaiah 30:15

[15] *This is what the Sovereign Lord, THE HOLY ONE OF ISRAEL, SAYS:*
"In repentance and rest is your salvation,
in quietness and trust is your strength.

Steady on Me.

You will keep in perfect peace if your mind is steadfast upon me. To keep your thoughts resolute on my purposes and stay unwavering seeking all that I have for you. Firm, loyal, and determined is the will of your mind and the attitude of your heart. Remain in my peace by remaining on me. Work hard to stay away from formulas and quick fixes that leave you worse off than when you begin. Stay steady on me. It's as simple and easy as that.

Isaiah 26:3

³ *You will keep in perfect peace*
those whose minds are steadfast,
because they trust in you.

Get Ready to be Soaked!

I want to fill you today like a bucket being filled to overflow as water gushes out and soaks everything around it. This is how I long to fill you up. So that from the inside out you are pouring out grace, love and peace to everyone around you. At times you may feel like your bucket is completely empty with nothing to give out. Ask me to come and fill up your bucket today that you may soak the world around you for this is what you're made for.

Song of Songs 2:10
[10] *My beloved spoke and said to me,*
"Arise, my darling,
my beautiful one, come with me.

My Voice Alone – Your Guide Forever.

With the presence of my voice you'll know which way to turn and how to move. It's my constant, steady, soft yet commanding voice which leads. No longer will systems and formulas be your guide but my voice alone. It will be louder, clearer, and more distant and come in forms which will bring your life and love. Tune in today and draw close to my voice – the source of life, love and much direction. Let it be the map which guides your life!

Jeremiah 6:16

¹⁶ *This is what the LORD SAYS:*
"Stand at the crossroads and look;
ask for the ancient paths,
ask where the good way is, and walk in it,
and you will find rest for your souls.

February
Devotional

Seek the Truth.

Be careful what you assume, so you do not move forward without proof of the matter. Maybe it's in dealing with a friend, a sticky situation, an issue with your spouse, or a circumstance in your family. Don't assume that you know everything when in fact you still don't have all the facts. Ask questions, dig a little deeper, and pursue the truth. Put your feelings and your own agenda aside and seek to be an honesty finder. Never assume what you in fact do not know.

_____

_____

_____

_____

_____

_____

_____

_____

_____

_____

Proverbs 4:7

⁷The beginning of wisdom is this: Get wisdom.
Though it cost all you have, get understanding.

You're Stronger than You Know.

I get it. You're tired. You're worn out. You're burned out on life, on friendships, even on family. You've had enough and you've all but thrown in the towel. This day I speak a new and fresh day over you, a new source of energy, life and determination. When you aren't sure if you can go any farther and aren't sure if you have what it takes, keep reaching and keep striving for there's more strength in you than you realize. There's more grit in you than you're aware. I see you and I see that you're stronger than you even know!

_____
_____
_____
_____
_____
_____
_____
_____
_____
_____
_____

James 1:12

12 Blessed is the one who perseveres under trial because, having stood the test, that person will receive the crown of life that the Lord has promised to those who love him.

Step Forward in Faith.

Sometimes faith looks like taking a nap. Sometimes faith looks like the next task on your to do list. Sometimes faith looks like serving on the school board. Sometimes faith looks like saying no, when you know they won't be happy. Sometimes faith means waiting patiently for the right answer. Faith looks different for everyone and in each circumstance. When you dial into my voice, you'll know if you're stepping out in faith or stepping forward in fear. Let me give you wisdom today on what faith looks like for you.

_____

_____

_____

_____

_____

_____

_____

_____

_____

_____

Proverbs 3:5-6
5 Trust in the LORD with all your heart
and lean not on your own understanding;
6 in all your ways submit to him,
and he will make your paths straight.

I Will Never Let You Go.

I will never let you go. When the storms come, and the waves seem to swallow you whole, I will never let you go. When tragedy comes at you and catches you off guard, I will never let you go. When the world is against you and chaos is all around, I will never let you go. When it seems like there's no one you can trust, I will never let you go. When it feels like the pressure of your surroundings is too much to bear, I will never let you go. When the rain never seems to stop, I will never let you go. Hear me today, I WILL NEVER LET YOU GO.

_____

_____

_____

_____

_____

_____

_____

_____

_____

_____

Psalm 18:1-2
1 I love you, LORD, my strength.
2 The LORD is my rock, my fortress and my deliverer;
my God is my rock, in whom I take refuge,
my shield and the horn of my salvation, my stronghold.

I am Ready to Meet You Today.

Without hesitation I will be there. To hold you up, to draw you close and to move you forward. Without hesitation I will run to your rescue. I will catch your fall and meet you right where you are. Without hesitation, I create the space for you to breathe, the space for you to run and the atmosphere for you to be fully you. Without hesitation I bless you with my abundance and provide your every need. Without hesitation I am here, always waiting and ready to meet with you today.

_____
_____
_____
_____
_____
_____
_____
_____
_____
_____

Psalm 18:28-29

28 You, LORD, keep my lamp burning;
my God turns my darkness into light.
29 With your help I can advance against a troop;
with my God I can scale a wall.

41

My Roots are Going Deep.

Your faithfulness I see, and I will reward you. Immediate gratification is not what I am about. Yes, I'll give you peace in the storm, and hope in the midst of anguish, but momentary pleasure is a fleeting reward. I am here for the long haul, the entirety of the race, giving you the perseverance and faith to keep you going long after others have quit. So, stay faithful today. I am building a deep reserve within you that is more powerful than any one-time quick fix. Keep going today and trust the strong foundation, which I am building within you!

_____
_____
_____
_____
_____
_____
_____
_____
_____
_____

Proverbs 3:3-4
³ Let love and faithfulness never leave you;
bind them around your neck,
write them on the tablet of your heart.
⁴ Then you will win favor and a good name
in the sight of God and man.

I am Meeting You in Every Decision Today.

With every decision I want to meet you there. At times you're quick to say yes, quick to say no, or maybe you can't decide either way. As decisions approach you today, seek me with where I am calling you to go, and whom I am entrusting you to be with. I've given you the authority and power to make wise and bold decisions. Connect with me and let me give you an ease in your answer.

_____

_____

_____

_____

_____

_____

_____

_____

_____

_____

_____

_____

James 3:17

*17 But the wisdom that comes from heaven is first
of all pure; then peace-loving, considerate, submissive,
full of mercy and good fruit, impartial and sincere.*

Run Today – A Little Farther & Faster.

Run today - a little farther, a little faster and with a little more determination. You're going places and seeking a destiny, which has your name written all over it. I give you permission to get excited and shout for JOY! Push yourself a little harder today because you have what it takes and what you need is already within you. I've called you to greatness and positioned you for amazing feats so go ahead and run a little more today. You have what it takes, and I am right there with you!

_____

_____

_____

_____

_____

_____

_____

_____

Hebrews 12:1-2

¹ Therefore, since we are surrounded by such a great
cloud of witnesses, let us throw off everything that hinders
and the sin that so easily entangles. And let us run with perseverance
the race marked out for us, ² fixing our eyes on Jesus, the pioneer and
perfecter of faith. For the joy set before him he endured the cross,
scorning its shame, and sat down at the right hand of the throne of God.

I am Calling You Out – Yes YOU!

I am calling you out – calling you further and farther than you've ever been. It may be uncomfortable, awkward and even a little scary, but know that this is me moving you on. Your good Father who has orchestrated these events for you, who you can trust that I am marking the road ahead with provision and abundant blessing. I'll never leave you and especially now as you are stepping out in new territory, know that I have covered every angle. You can trust I am the one pushing you forward! So, go for it!

_____

_____

_____

_____

_____

_____

_____

_____

Deuteronomy 8:6-9
⁶ Observe the commands of the LORD your God, walking in obedience to him and revering him. ⁷ For the LORD your God is bringing you into a good land — a land with brooks, streams, and deep springs gushing out into the valleys and hills; ⁸ a land with wheat and barley; vines and fig trees, pomegranates, olive oil and honey; ⁹ a land where bread will not be scarce and you will lack nothing; a land where the rocks are iron and you can dig copper out of the hills.

Rush Your Responsibilities Right Back to Me!

With the rush of a new day comes the rush of responsibilities. You feel the weight, the burden, and the heaviness of all you have to do, but I am with you for this very purpose! The reality is you live above your problems, and you carry the power to rise above them. I am meeting you today in the midst of all you have to carry, showing you that I am the one who always wanted to carry them for you. As soon as the day rushes in, rush your responsibilities right back to me!

_____

_____

_____

_____

_____

_____

_____

_____

_____

Isaiah 41:10

¹⁰ So do not fear, for I am with you;
do not be dismayed, for I am your God.
I will strengthen you and help you;
I will uphold you with my righteous right hand.

I Cover You.

Like a wool coat in winter, I keep you warm in the dead of night. In the worst rain storms, I keep you dry. I cover you. I cover your family, friends, community, job, and commitments. I am here as your protector like a blanket over your life I protect you. It may seem as if there's no telling the chaos that could come in and wreak havoc on your life, but I am here to protect you in all areas of your life from the smallest of details to the most significant. I AM your great protector.

Proverbs 2:7-8

[7] He holds success in store for the upright,
he is a shield to those whose walk is blameless,
[8] for he guards the course of the just
and protects the way of his faithful ones.

It's All About Perspective.

Looking around it may seem like the grass really is greener on the other side, as promotions are happening at every turn and it seem like you are left in the dust. Yet, you my child, have full access to the resources of Heaven. You have a Father whose ready to pour out His abundance upon you. When you feel less than those around you, this is where I show up and show off for you – giving you what you need at the proper time. I won't pour out more than you can handle and will be sure to keep your grass green and growing. The grass really is greener on *your* side.

_____

_____

_____

_____

_____

_____

_____

_____

_____

_____

_____

_____

Romans 8:28

28 And we know that in all things God works for the good of those who love him, who have been called according to his purpose.

Enjoy All of Me Today!

With one word everything changes. With one command, my army of angels flock to help you. With one swoop of my hand I take care of you and you see the fullness of who I am. With one breathe upon your life, love rushes in to save you. With one touch, every bit of you is healed inside and out. The good news is you don't get one part of me, but ALL of me. So, enjoy the fullness of who I am today, it's yours to receive!

_____

_____

_____

_____

_____

_____

_____

_____

_____

_____

_____

_____

_____

1 John 4:9-10

⁹ This is how God showed his love among us: He sent his one and only Son into the world that we might live through him.
¹⁰ This is love: not that we loved God, but that he loved us and sent his Son as an atoning sacrifice for our sins.

A Day of Love.

A day of love focused on one another and the ones you hold so dear. This day as you look to bless, pour out, and give something special to those who hold dear, desire to see them and understand them inside and out today. Take the time to honor them, appreciate them, and love on them beyond your normal gesture. This requires thought of the heart and mind, so that when you give it comes from a place of understanding, insight and great compassion. To truly love is to see them fully and then love them all the more.

_____

_____

_____

_____

_____

_____

_____

_____

_____

_____

_____

_____

_____

John 3:16

[16] *For God so loved the world that he gave his one and only Son, that whoever believes in him shall not perish but have eternal life.*

Steward Well What I Entrust to You.

I take what you have, and I multiply it. You may look around at your resources, at the things you own and even your bank account and it may look bare, with each day feeling as if you "own" less and less. But I am your Father who seeks to add, bless, and multiply all you have. Be a good steward of what I have entrusted to you and you'll begin to see an overwhelming abundance in the blessings I pour out to you. I don't operate in the world's standards, but I operate in faith, hope and love. Keep walking in these dimensions and you'll find you have all you need!

_____

_____

_____

_____

_____

_____

_____

_____

_____

_____

_____

_____

John 15:7

*⁷ If you remain in me and my words remain in you,
ask whatever you wish, and it will be done for you.*

My Faithfulness Never Leaves You.

My faithfulness never leaves you. It greets you in the morning; it rushes in to save you throughout the day and tucks you in at night. I am faithful to your every need. I am faithful to the friends, family and relationships around you. I am faithful at your workplace and with the tasks you must complete. I am faithful when the world around you falls apart. I am faithful in the storm and in the sunshine. It is my faithfulness you can bet on. Look for my faithfulness and you'll see it all around you.

_____

_____

_____

_____

_____

_____

_____

_____

_____

_____

_____

_____

Psalm 91:4
⁴He will cover you with his feathers,
and under his wings you will find refuge;
his faithfulness will be your shield and rampart.

I'll Get You Through This Day.

Keep the faith they say but what does that even mean? To have faith, to have hope, and to keep going when life doesn't make sense. There's no formula, no rules, or no set designs for how to maintain and sustain a life of faith, hope and love. In these moments of despair, faith is the last word on your mind, as you wonder how you can keep going? Walking out in faith comes in the little moments where you get out of bed, make that phone call, and choose joy when all you have is tears. I'll give you this faith my friends. Just keep asking and I'll get you through this day.

_____

_____

_____

_____

_____

_____

_____

_____

Psalm 23:4

4 Even though I walk
through the darkest valley,
I will fear no evil,
for you are with me;
your rod and your staff,
they comfort me.

Thanks and Praise.

Thanks, and praise. Thanks, and praise. Thanks, and praise. When you don't know what to do, which direction to go, or how to move forward thanks and praise is always the best way. Make your list of gratitude; think through your declarations of praise and speak them, write them, and re-read them again and again. Let these words awaken truth to your soul and bring hope to your mind that you would remember my faithfulness to you. When thanks and praise are the heartbeat of your days, hope becomes the cadence of your heart and gives you the strength to carry on.

_____

_____

_____

_____

_____

_____

_____

_____

_____

_____

Psalm 69:30

*30 I will praise God's name in song
and glorify him with thanksgiving.*

Stay Steady on My Voice.

Y ou are moving even when you feel like you're at a standstill. Where you're headed is set for you and marked for your destiny. Your bones are marked by determination and tenacity. There's no quit in you and when moments come that look hopeless and you wonder if you can move forward, you'll draw back to me and my voice which will show you the way forward and the direction you must go. Stay steady on my voice and you won't miss a beat.

_____

_____

_____

_____

_____

_____

_____

_____

_____

_____

_____

_____

_____

_____

Psalm 18:30

[30] *As for God, his way is perfect:*
The LORD's word is flawless;
he shields all who take refuge in him.

My Perfect Provision at the Perfect Time.

You can trust that I am giving you everything you need when you need it. When it's time to run I'll give you your running shoes. When it's time to swim I'll give you your flippers. When it's time to bike, I'll give you the 10 speed. Don't forget if you have a bike when it's time to swim then it will only weigh you down, and if you have flippers when you want to run, you'll only fall on your face. Trust in my perfect provision at my perfect time. Don't get caught in what others around you are getting, I see and know just what YOU need when YOU need it!

_____

_____

_____

_____

_____

_____

_____

_____

_____

Psalm 37:3-4

³ Trust in the LORD and do good;
dwell in the land and enjoy safe pasture.
⁴ Take delight in the LORD,
and he will give you the desires of your heart.

Stay Alert. Stay Prepared. Stay Ready.

Stay alert, stay prepared, stay ready because at the proper time, I will advance your position and draw the right people your way. I see your efforts and I will pour out my faithfulness to you. Stay diligent to the task and remain focused on the purposes I have for you and keep your eyes intently on the agenda of Heaven. Every day, I am building your resolve, and fueling your determination knowing with each promotion you'll be ready.

Ephesians 6:18

[18] And pray in the Spirit on all occasions with all kinds of prayers and requests. With this in mind, be alert and always keep on praying for all the Lord's people.

I Will Take Care of You.

I will take care of you. When the world throws every obstacle in your face, I will take care of you. When your friends are too busy to see you need a helping hand, I will take care of you. When your family is rushing from one activity to the next, I will take care of you. When your coworkers are caught up in their own agenda, I will take care of you. I see your needs today, I understand your desires, and as your Creator I know just what you need. Let me take care of you today.

Psalm 91:15-16

[15] *He will call on me, and I will answer him;*
I will be with him in trouble,
I will deliver him and honor him.
[16] *With long life I will satisfy him*
and show him my salvation."

With Each Step You're Getting Stronger.

With every step, you're getting stronger and moving further down the track. Your stride might not always look pretty or graceful and it may not feel like you're even moving forward but trust me this day you are advancing. Your steps no matter how big or small, are pushing you towards your goal. Don't spend hours looking back, but keep your eyes straight head as you gaze at your future. Only then will you glance back from time to time to see how far you've come and how far I've taken you. Then you'll have the energy to move with greater speed.

Hebrews 2:1

¹ *We must pay the most careful attention, therefore, to what we have heard, so that we do not drift away.*

Where Will Your Focus Be Today?

W here will your focus be today? Will you choose to narrow your focus on me? Will you dial in on what's true, good, right, and pure? Your ability to focus on what's most important is what gives your heart, soul, body, and mind a greater purpose. Align your focus with me today, as you stay sustained on my words, my nature, and the heartbeat of who I am. Keep your eyes on the prize and you'll never lose your step, you won't miss a beat, and you'll glance back and be amazed at how far you've come. Just remember it's all in your focus!

_____

_____

_____

_____

_____

_____

_____

Jeremiah 32:38-41

[38] *They will be my people, and I will be their God.* [39] *I will give them singleness of heart and action, so that they will always fear me and that all will then go well for them and for their children after them.* [40] *I will make an everlasting covenant with them: I will never stop doing good to them, and I will inspire them to fear me, so that they will never turn away from me.* [41] *I will rejoice in doing them good and will assuredly plant them in this land with all my heart and soul.*

You Decide How You'll Live Today!

Don't rely on your feelings today. You aren't meant to live at the command of every passing emotion. Don't ride the emotional roller coaster of life, fearful of every next turn. Stay steadfast on my truth, on my promises, and watch how your emotions will align with how I see you and how I see your circumstances. You may feel like you are ruled by your feelings and that they even direct your day, but this isn't so. Declare OUT LOUD today the emotional state you long to live in, and then believe it, and act accordingly. Your negative feelings don't define you; you decide how you'll live today!

_____
_____
_____
_____
_____
_____
_____
_____
_____
_____
_____

2 Corinthians 5:17

_17 Therefore, if anyone is in Christ, the new creation has come:
The old has gone, the new is here!_

I am Your Help.

I am your help. Your help in time of great need and even basic every day needs. I'll help you with the little things, the big things, and everything in between. I am your help. I provide services, resources, and solutions to the questions in your head, and the problems that surround you. I usher in people who have what you need, and I welcome opportunities in your life that provide answers to what seems impossible. I am your help today, come to me, and ask for my help. I am here, I am ready, and help is not only on its way, but right here by your side.

_____

_____

_____

_____

_____

_____

_____

_____

_____

_____

_____

Psalm 124:8
⁸ Our help is in the name of the LORD,
the Maker of heaven and earth.

Today I am Your Routine.

Today I am your routine, I am your breakthrough, and I am the one who will get you through the day. I am the one who sustains you in the chaos, and the one who calms your deepest, darkest fears. I am the one who helps you when you need it the most, and I am the one who provides you a house when you just wanted a raincoat. I am the one, who gives you an answer when you've been praying all night. I am the one you can count on when you all you want is a hug. For I AM the great I AM and you can count on me this day.

Exodus 3:13-15

13 *Moses said to God, "Suppose I go to the Israelites and say to them, 'The God of your fathers has sent me to you,' and they ask me, 'What is his name?' Then what shall I tell them?"*
14 *God said to Moses, "I AM WHO I AM. This is what you are to say to the Israelites: 'I AM has sent me to you.'"*

No More Looking Back – Only Forward!

It's time to break off your rear-view mirrors and run forward. You've spent too much time recounting memories and the seemingly better days of old. This is the time to run forward and keep your target on the opportunities ahead. Looking back with an attitude of regret only keeps you locked up in the past, holding you prisoner to the former days. Be thankful for what was, then move in faith for what will be. Don't let your rear-view mirrors define you today. Just look ahead and see the beauty of the what's in front of you!

_____

_____

_____

_____

_____

_____

_____

_____

Isaiah 43:18-19

[18] *"Forget the former things;*
do not dwell on the past.
[19] *See, I am doing a new thing!*
Now it springs up; do you not perceive it?
I am making a way in the wilderness
and streams in the wasteland.

March
Devotional

One Focus and One Direction is All You Need.

One focus and one direction are all you need. Multiple directions will leave you confused and flustered with too many irons in the fire as you try to juggle every single plate. Tune into me and I'll show you which commitments to lie down, which irons to set aside, and which plates to put back in the cabinet. It's time to narrow our focus, trusting that I'll take care of the rest.

_____

_____

_____

_____

_____

_____

_____

_____

_____

_____

_____

_____

_____

_____

Matthew 6:33

*33 But seek first his kingdom and his righteousness,
and all these things will be given to you as well.*

It's Time to Start a Fresh!

From time to time you must clear the canvas and start a fresh. I want you to remember there's a clear path in front of you and you are the creator. Yes, I am here to guide you and help you every step of the way, but I will not micromanage you. I've given you gifts, talents, and abilities, and placed creativity within you and around you. Step out today and begin painting, adding color and shaping the world in front of you. Trusting that with every stroke, you're one step closer to where you want to be.

_____
_____
_____
_____
_____
_____
_____
_____
_____
_____
_____
_____

Luke 5:27-28
*27 After this, Jesus went out and saw a tax collector by the
name of Levi sitting at his tax booth. "Follow me," Jesus said to him,
28 and Levi got up, left everything and followed him.*

Just Do the Next Thing.

Let love and faithfulness never leave you. Grab onto them when your boat is about to capsize. Grab onto to them when the storms of life comes at you. Grab onto them when you aren't sure who your friends are. Grab onto love and let faithfulness be your guide. "What should I be faithful to? Who should I love?" Just look at the one in front of you. It's the easy and simple guide of life when nothing else makes sense.

_____

_____

_____

_____

_____

_____

_____

_____

_____

_____

_____

_____

_____

Mark 12:30-31

[30] *Love the Lord your God with all your heart and with all your soul and with all your mind and with all your strength.*[a]
[31] *The second is this: 'Love your neighbor as yourself.'*[b]
There is no commandment greater than these."

I'll Come Like the Wind &
Give You the Solution.

There are so many decisions, so many questions, and so many choices in a day. Wondering, waiting, and having to take action all in the same breath. It's exhausting, overwhelming and you may just want to run from the world. You wonder who will miss me? Will anybody care? Yet it's this very place and position, which I have called you and set you in. You must only take a breath and ask me for my wisdom. I'll come like the wind and give you your solution.

_____
_____
_____
_____
_____
_____
_____
_____
_____

John 14:26-27

26 But the Advocate, the Holy Spirit, whom the Father will send in my name, will teach you all things and will remind you of everything I have said to you. 27 Peace I leave with you; my peace I give you. I do not give to you as the world gives. Do not let your hearts be troubled and do not be afraid.

70

My Grace Surrounds You.

Know that I've not only given you grace for today but grace for every moment throughout the day. If you have a task to complete, an assignment to finish or someone to meet with, I have you covered. There's favor on your day and favor on every move you make because I have your back. As you dive into your agenda know that grace will meet you at every turn. You may wonder how you'll get through this day, but you need not worry for my grace is already there, already surrounding you, and ready to give you what you need.

_____

_____

_____

_____

_____

_____

_____

_____

_____

_____

_____

_____

2 Corinthians 12:9

⁹ But he said to me, "My grace is sufficient for you, for my power is made perfect in weakness." Therefore, I will boast all the more gladly about my weaknesses, so that Christ's power may rest on me.

My Faithfulness Will Never Leave You.

I am faithful to the core, faithful to the bone, and faithful to your every move. You can't make a mistake; you can't make a wrong turn, because my faithfulness covers every move you make. Look to me with delight, look to me with assurance because my loyalty will show up for you day after day. My promises are the heartbeat of who I am, and nothing can take that away from you. Let your confidence rise in the truth that my faithfulness will never leave you and you can rest in this truth.

_____

_____

_____

_____

_____

_____

_____

_____

_____

_____

Matthew 17:20

*[20] He replied, "Because you have so little faith. Truly I tell you,
if you have faith as small as a mustard seed, you can say
to this mountain, 'Move from here to there,' and it will move.
Nothing will be impossible for you."*

Stay the Course & Keep Going!

With every step you're gaining confidence, clarity and insight into the next season. It may seem like you're taking one step forward and two steps back but it's the tortoise that wins the race. Day by day you're gaining traction, doing the little things, which actually breed big results. Stay the course; keep going, and never waiver from the narrow path in front of you. If it were easy, everyone would do it. You weren't made for the wide path, but you're destined for something amazing, specific and unique. This is your day – seize it!

John 15: 1-4

"I am the true vine, and my Father is the gardener. [2] He cuts off every branch in me that bears no fruit, while every branch that does bear fruit he prunes[a] so that it will be even more fruitful. [3] You are already clean because of the word I have spoken to you. [4] Remain in me, as I also remain in you. No branch can bear fruit by itself; it must remain in the vine. Neither can you bear fruit unless you remain in me.

Look with My Eyes.

The path of least resistance may seem easy, may seem comfortable, and may seem like it's the best option in front of you, but is it? Look closely, look again, and look with my eyes. Be careful of the ways that seem too good to be true and are filled with sweet morsels. Look again, look closely and look with my eyes. The path of least resistance isn't how the pearl gets formed. Look again and look closely for I am paving the road in front of you and it's designed to give you all you need.

_____

_____

_____

_____

_____

_____

_____

_____

_____

_____

_____

James 1:2-4

2 Consider it pure joy, my brothers and sisters,[a] whenever you face trials of many kinds, 3 because you know that the testing of your faith produces perseverance. 4 Let perseverance finish its work so that you may be mature and complete, not lacking anything.

You Have What It Takes to Keep Fighting.

You're stronger than you think, more courageous than you can imagine and you have what it takes to keep fighting. At times it can feel like you can barely move and can't remember left from right, but remember you're stronger than you think, and carry faith that can move mountains. This is who you are and this is what you stand for. You're stronger than you think and more courageous than you can imagine.

_____

_____

_____

_____

_____

_____

_____

_____

_____

_____

_____

Deuteronomy 31:7

⁷ Then Moses summoned Joshua and said to him in the presence of all Israel, "Be strong and courageous, for you must go with this people into the land that the LORD swore to their ancestors to give them, and you must divide it among them as their inheritance.

I am Never Leaving You, Never Forsaking You.

I am with you, just as the wind is on your face. You can't see it, but you can feel it and sense it all around you. I am guiding you, directing you, and giving you nudges as to the way you should go, and when it's time to stop, to rest, and put your feet up I am there as well. Sitting with you, and giving your soul the deep rest, it needs. Remember in your sitting, standing, and sprinting forward, I am there - never leaving you and never forsaking you. Just as the wind is all around, I am here too.

Deuteronomy 31:6

⁶ Be strong and courageous. Do not be afraid or terrified because of them, for the LORD your God goes with you; he will never leave you nor forsake you."

Let My Goodness & Grace Mark Your Life.

There are some things you can't make up, some things in life that are clearly marked by my goodness and my grace. Situations and circumstances that are clearly set apart by my faithfulness in your life. Stay on the look out for these times and these moments as they happen more often than you realize. Let me wake you up today to those instances where nothing else and no one else could be responsible for the blessings in your life. I operate in the big and little things - goodness so great that you just can't make up!

_____

_____

_____

_____

_____

_____

_____

_____

Psalm 118:5-7

⁵ When hard pressed, I cried to the LORD;
he brought me into a spacious place.
⁶ The LORD is with me; I will not be afraid.
What can mere mortals do to me?
⁷ The LORD is with me; he is my helper.
I look in triumph on my enemies.

77

Know that I am God.

There are some battles you are not meant to fight, for I alone will bring you the victory. Without lifting a finger, you will see the defeat of your greatest enemies both inside and out. It may be hard to pull up your bootstraps and charge ahead but this time you must sit, rest and trust that I will take care of you. Now is not the time to shrink back in fear wondering if I'll come through, now is the time to sit in your chair, sip on your coffee and know that I am God.

_____

_____

_____

_____

_____

_____

_____

_____

_____

_____

Psalm 37:7

*⁷ Be still before the LORD
and wait patiently for him;
do not fret when people succeed in their ways,
when they carry out their wicked schemes.*

This is Your Time to Shine!

Don't forget to walk with a swagger. Yes, you heard me right. To walk with a defined confidence knowing whose child you are and what qualities you carry. You have authority, you have power, and you have what it takes. Hold your head up high and look straight ahead because you have so much to be proud of, and so much for which I am proud of you. Strut your stuff for this is your time to shine! I've made you for greatness.

_____

_____

_____

_____

_____

_____

_____

_____

_____

_____

_____

Colossians 3:23-24

²³ Whatever you do, work at it with all your heart,
as working for the Lord, not for human masters,
²⁴ since you know that you will receive an inheritance
from the Lord as a reward. It is the
Lord Christ you are serving.

I am Building a Legacy which Lasts!

The world wants to hand you its quick and easy fix for the day, but that's not how true success comes to your life. You might be looking for a drive thru to collect all that you need but often you are looking for the wrong instant solution, when in fact I am paving the way for you – day by day, moment by moment giving you everything you need at the proper time, so you can build something magnificent. A legacy that stands the test of time!

_____

_____

_____

_____

_____

_____

_____

_____

_____

_____

_____

_____

Isaiah 57:14
14 And it will be said:
"Build up, build up, prepare the road!
Remove the obstacles out of the way of my people."

You're Stepping into the New!

Y ou have launched forward and advanced into new territory, new spaces and new places. You are doing it and I could not be prouder of you. One foot in front of the other you forge ahead creating a new path. The new season is upon you and I am equipping you with the tools you need. "Out with the old and in with the new," I say. Wake up to the freshness of this hour – there are NEW things ahead!

_____

_____

_____

_____

_____

_____

_____

_____

_____

_____

_____

_____

_____

_____

Joshua 1:9

[9] Have I not commanded you? Be strong and courageous.
Do not be afraid; do not be discouraged, for the
LORD your God will be with you wherever you go."

81

Pile Upon Pile My Goodness Will Come.

My goodness will come. Layer upon layer I will pour out my abundance upon you and cover you with my sweet blessings. Look for them, wait for them, watch for them, and prepare for them. They will heap upon your life and advance towards you, your family and your friends. Seek me in the light and in the dark and you'll notice my every move upon your life and see that it's covered with my goodness.

_____

_____

_____

_____

_____

_____

_____

_____

_____

_____

_____

_____

_____

Psalm 16:2-3

2 I say to the Lord, "You are my Lord;
apart from you I have no good thing."
3 I say of the holy people who are in the land,
"They are the noble ones in whom is all my delight."

I am Building a Resolve to Stand the Storms.

Patience, my friend, patience. It's easier said than done I know – to set aside your emotions, to move past your anger and frustration and to trust in the unraveling of the events around you. Accepting and tolerating the delay while still moving forward. This patience is building your character and resolve which will stand the storms and, in the end, you'll look back and see the steady foundation created in you AND around you. Patience, my friend patience.

_____

_____

_____

_____

_____

_____

_____

_____

_____

_____

_____

James 5:7-8

⁷ Be patient, then, brothers and sisters, until the Lord's coming.
See how the farmer waits for the land to yield its valuable crop,
patiently waiting for the autumn and spring rains. ⁸ You too,
be patient and stand firm, because the Lord's coming is near.

When Nothing Makes Sense
I am There.

When you want to escape to a faraway island, I am there. When you want to hide and bury your face, I am there. When the world is coming at you, I am there. When you want to crawl into a hole and never return, I am there. Now and always, I am there. When sadness, anger, and exhaustion find you, I am there. When voices are shouting at you from every angle, I am there. Again, and again I am there, guiding you and drawing you back into my heart, allowing the world to makes sense again.

_____

_____

_____

_____

_____

_____

_____

_____

_____

Isaiah 46:4

4 Even to your old age and gray hairs
I am he, I am he who will sustain you.
I have made you and I will carry you;
I will sustain you and I will rescue you.

I Love You, I Love You, I Love You.

I love you, I love you, I love you. I love you when others don't. I love you when you make a mess. I love you without any hooks or any limitations. I don't put up walls; I don't withhold good gifts from you and I never tire of looking for ways to lavish my blessings on your life. I am a steady rock, a steady force, and a constant source you can rely on again and again. Don't doubt my goodness towards you. I love you, I love you, I love you and nothing, and absolutely nothing can take that away. Live in this reality today.

_____

_____

_____

_____

_____

_____

_____

_____

_____

_____

1 Corinthians 13:4-7

⁴ Love is patient, love is kind. It does not envy, it does not boast,
it is not proud. ⁵ It does not dishonor others, it is not self-seeking,
it is not easily angered, it keeps no record of wrongs. ⁶ Love does
not delight in evil but rejoices with the truth. ⁷ It always protects,
always trusts, always hopes, always perseveres.

Listen, Listen, and Then Listen Some More.

Seek first to understand then to be understood. First listen, ask questions, and probe into the heart and mind of those around you. Make sure you have all the facts, and all the relevant information you need so you have the appropriate response, the right attitude, and the correct action forward. Judging too quickly you'll make a mess, and by acting rash you will cause hurt feelings. Seek first to fully understand all the pieces that are in play and only then will you be understood.

_____

_____

_____

_____

_____

_____

_____

_____

_____

_____

_____

Psalm 130:5

⁵ *I wait for the LORD, my whole being waits,*
and in his word I put my hope.

Stay the Course and Keep Steady on the Path.

Stay the course, keep steady on the path and keep your eyes focused on the goal. Moaning and groaning with every step will only make the journey more difficult and more strenuous. Keeping positive people and positive reinforcement around you is crucial to your success. Be resilient when the adventure is less than desirable, be tenacious when it feels like you can't hang on any longer and go one more step when it seems like you just can't go any further. Stay the course, for there are good things ahead!

Proverbs 16:3

3 Commit to the LORD whatever you do,
and he will establish your plans.

You are the Masterpiece!

Be careful how you create your life. Don't rush from this thing to that thing, not taking time to notice the details. At the same time don't move too slowly getting bogged down by every meaningless detail as if it's the cornerstone in which you build. Instead move carefully, steadily, and consistently adding and subtracting as you see fit. No need to worry as to what will come next or what it will look like, just keep building and trusting that I am helping you create a masterpiece – understanding that actually the masterpiece is YOU!

\
\
\
\
\
\
\
\
\
\
\
\
\
\

Psalm 36:9

⁹ For with you is the fountain of life;
in your light we see light.

True Love – To Give Expecting Nothing in Return.

The minute you give your time, talents & treasures expecting to get something in return is the minute you've missed the chance to truly love. To give without regret, to love with no strings attached, and to pour out your life as if you've got nothing to lose. This is a life worth living. To know it and say it is one thing but to live it is quite another. It's here where you give so freely and you've all but forgotten the effort it took. You just know once again today is a new day and you're ready to give again...expecting nothing in return.

---

2 Corinthians 8:5

[5] *And they exceeded our expectations: They gave themselves first of all to the Lord, and then by the will of God also to us.*

You Can and You Will Make It!

Everyday seems like a fight, a struggle, and at times a battle you aren't equipped for. You wonder if you can go on, if you have what it takes, and your mind spirals out of control, "Is it worth it? Will I make it? Am I failing?" With more questions than answers you want to throw in the towel and call it quits BUT let me urge you today to listen in a little closer to the strong, growing voice of strength within you which says, "You can, and you will!" Keep fighting because it is worth it. You will make it. This I can promise you.

_____

_____

_____

_____

_____

_____

_____

_____

_____

_____

Psalm 37:23-24

*23 The LORD makes firm the steps
of the one who delights in him;
24 though he may stumble, he will not fall,
for the LORD upholds him with his hand.*

Stay Steady on the Task.

When the plant begins to sprout you shout to your friend, "We did it, it's growing," But a week later you return seeing nothing but a brown lifeless leaf wondering what happened? So quickly you forgot when you birth something new it takes time, endurance, and consistent nurturing. You may see growth early on but that is only an indication that more time, energy and attention is needed to see more progress. Keep your eyes focused and your hands diligent to the task and you'll never regret your patient endurance in those first days.

_____

_____

_____

_____

_____

Psalm 40:1-3

¹ *I waited patiently for the LORD;*
he turned to me and heard my cry.
² *He lifted me out of the slimy pit,*
out of the mud and mire;
he set my feet on a rock
and gave me a firm place to stand.
³ *He put a new song in my mouth,*
a hymn of praise to our God.
Many will see and fear the LORD
and put their trust in him.

91

Let Me Speak to Rest to Your Roller Coaster Emotions.

Emotions. Yours are everywhere - up, down and everywhere in between. Some days you aren't sure what you're feeling, why you're feeling it, or where "it" came from. "Am I losing my mind?" you wonder. As you battle the torment in your mind and ride the emotional roller coaster ask me to give you clarity, direction and allow yourself to just sit for a while. I'll cut through those feelings and take you off the roller coaster you never wanted to ride.

_____

_____

_____

_____

_____

_____

_____

_____

Psalm 84:5-7

⁵ *Blessed are those whose strength is in you,*
whose hearts are set on pilgrimage.
⁶ *As they pass through the Valley of Baka,*
they make it a place of springs;
the autumn rains also cover it with pools.[a]
⁷ *They go from strength to strength,*
till each appears before God in Zion.

A Confidence in Me will Never Let You Down.

B e confident I say. Yes, be confident, bold and daring, but be careful where your confidence comes from. Does it come from your own doing, your own strength, and your own ability, which puffs up and puffs out? Let me promise you no one is attracted to this false self-confidence and you will only fool yourself for so long. Put your confidence in what I've given you, what I am pouring out to you and stand up tall in which I've created you to be! This is confidence you can always rely and will never let you down!

Jeremiah 1:17

[17] *"Get yourself ready! Stand up and say to them whatever I command you. Do not be terrified by them.*

Trust Me with the Whole of Your Heart.

Trust me with the whole of your life and the whole of your heart. There's nowhere you can run where I am not there and nowhere you can hide where I will not find you. I am not seeking you in order to enforce the rules or lay down the hammer. I am seeking you with my entire heart ready to give you what you need. As a parent desires the absolute best for their child, I too want to give you the world. It's when you turn and decide to give me the whole of your heart when you realize you truly have it all.

_____

_____

_____

_____

_____

_____

_____

_____

_____

_____

Psalm 40:4

⁴ Blessed is the one
who trusts in the LORD,
who does not look to the proud,
to those who turn aside to false gods.[a]

Show Me Today.

Show me where you want me to go and I'll be right there. Show me who you want me to be with and I'll run to meet them. Show me what you've committed my hands to do and I'll dive right in. Show me what my ears should entertain and I'll cut out the other noise. Show me this today and everyday after, for my heart longs to go a different way, my ears long to be tickled, and my eyes seem to swayed by all the flashy lights. Show me today Lord, for I don't want to know any other way.

_____

_____

_____

_____

_____

_____

_____

_____

_____

_____

_____

Psalm 86:11
11 Teach me your way, Lord,
that I may rely on your faithfulness;
give me an undivided heart,
that I may fear your name.

Be You – Be Original – The World is Waiting!

It's time for you to start being the real you. The you that lives fully, laughs freely and doesn't think twice about the things you shouldn't think twice about. "Be you," I say! "Be you!" There is nobody else like you. You're an original and anyone else you'd try to be would be a copycat! As you step out and step up, I can promise you won't regret this bold move and in fact you might even enjoy it! So, go on and be you today - the real you which the world can't wait to see!

Jeremiah 1:10

¹⁰See, today I appoint you over nations and kingdoms to uproot and tear down, to destroy and overthrow, to build and to plant."

Grab onto the Promises which are Yours!

With the hope of a new day the world is at your fingertips. Opportunity, advancement, peace, wisdom, provision and joy are all standing at your door waiting for you to invite them in. It's a choice, a decision, and a conscious action to say yes to the promises, which I have already placed around you and within you. Look for these fruits in your life, but don't just look open them up as gifts before you. Don't let today be just another day in which you wait, but rather look up knowing these gifts are yours to grab!

_____

_____

_____

_____

_____

_____

_____

_____

_____

_____

_____

Hebrews 6:11-12

[11] We want each of you to show this same diligence to the very end, so that what you hope for may be fully realized. [12] We do not want you to become lazy, but to imitate those who through faith and patience inherit what has been promised.

April
Devotional

Build Your Mind Up!

W hen the worst junk passes through your mind remember that doesn't define you and isn't how I see you. Be quick to dismiss these thoughts for they will eventually shape your life and become the essence of your days if you allow them. I gave you your mind as a powerful tool, a weapon against the enemy to build yourself up and to remind yourself of whose you are. Take captive every thought that doesn't scream positive hope and encouragement because soon they will become your everyday reality, eventually to define you.

_____

_____

_____

_____

_____

_____

_____

_____

_____

_____

_____

2 Corinthians 10:5

⁵ *We demolish arguments and every pretension that sets itself
up against the knowledge of God, and we take captive every
thought to make it obedient to Christ.*

In My Perfect Timing & Provision I Will Come!

Y ou're wondering, worrying, and trying to fill every void in your life with what seems right, normal, and good, but be careful with what you add to your life. Jesus too was tempted with seemingly "good" things and if chosen they would have brought him destruction. What seems right in the eyes of the world may be completely off in the Kingdom, so tread lightly, walk with discernment and look for my handprint as you move about your day. In my perfect timing and my perfect provision, I will come to fill and add to your life.

_____

_____

_____

_____

_____

_____

_____

_____

_____

_____

_____

_____

John 14:6
⁶Jesus answered, "I am the way and the truth and the life.
No one comes to the Father except through me.

Take Time for Space.

Sometimes there's space. Space to think, move, and breathe in order to allow my purposes to fill your days before people, tasks, and clutter get in the way. Resist the urge fill up your calendar just to make yourself busy. I know this moment of pause in your life is uncomfortable and awkward, but these are the places where I long to move, act, and add to your life. Let me come and fill this space in front of you as I create something from seemingly nothing. You'll be glad you stopped, noticed the pause and took time to enjoy the space!

Psalm 18:18-19

¹⁸ They confronted me in the day of my disaster,
but the LORD was my support.
¹⁹ He brought me out into a spacious place;
he rescued me because he delighted in me.

I am So Incredibly Proud of You!

When all you want to do is crawl into a hole, I am proud of you. When all your feelings scream pain and torment, I am proud of you. When chaos grips you on every side, I am proud of you. When you spoke, and you should have listened, I am proud of you. You my dear are perfect just as you are, and I am so very proud of you. I enjoy you; delight over you, and my eyes can't stop staring at you. My love is full, rich and abundant for you. Sit with me awhile, let me enjoy your company a little longer, because I couldn't be more pleased with you!

_____

_____

_____

_____

_____

_____

_____

_____

_____

_____

Psalm 110:1

¹ The LORD says to my lord: [a]

"Sit at my right hand

until I make your enemies

a footstool for your feet."

But the Greatest of These is Love.

Faith, hope and love but the greatest of these is love. You know it's true, you know the verse, you know the right answer, but I desire to move this reality from your head to heart. From your heart springs the energy of life, giving you the ability to receive and give all that I have so this love overflow becomes your everyday reality. Trust in who I am, hope in the greater picture, put your faith in what is unseen but never, never forget that love rests on all of these.

_____

_____

_____

_____

_____

_____

_____

_____

_____

_____

1 Corinthians 13:12-13

[12] *For now we see only a reflection as in a mirror; then we shall see face to face. Now I know in part; then I shall know fully, even as I am fully known.*
[13] *And now these three remain: faith, hope and love. But the greatest of these is love.*

I Take Care of Your Heart.

Don't forget you are in a process and a journey that takes patience and steadfast endurance. It's a moment by moment, day by day pursuit, which you can trust I am with you every step of the way. Allow this truth to be "enough" today. When you're not sure if you, others, or the world around you is enough, know that I am here and taking care of your heart. Let that be enough for today when nothing else will do.

_____

_____

_____

_____

_____

_____

_____

_____

_____

_____

Colossians 1:10-12
[10] so that you may live a life worthy of the Lord and please
him in every way: bearing fruit in every good work, growing in the
knowledge of God, [11] being strengthened with all power according to
his glorious might so that you may have great endurance and patience,
[12] and giving joyful thanks to the Father, who has qualified you[a] to
share in the inheritance of his holy people in the kingdom of light.

Let Go. Let Go. Let Go.

Let go of the expectations, demands, and those should have's, must of's, and absolutes you dump on your life. They are only weighing you down and causing you more harm than good. One after another they pile up and remind you that you don't measure up and everyone else is succeeding when you are failing miserably. WRONG! This is not your reality. Everyday you're following my voice while staying faithful and obedient to my leading - this what you must remember. No more weights on your shoulders. You're flying, my friend.

_____

_____

_____

_____

_____

_____

_____

_____

Psalm 119:5-7

⁵Oh, that my ways were steadfast
in obeying your decrees!
⁶Then I would not be put to shame
when I consider all your commands.
⁷I will praise you with an upright heart
as I learn your righteous laws.

Let Me Shine Light on Your True Reality.

Just because you believe it doesn't mean it's true. Test your thoughts. Put them up to the light and see if they hold up. Align them with my word and my voice and see if they match. You think something and feel something so strongly it can be hard to see the forest from the trees. Test your thoughts today and discern the trees from the forest and let me shed light on your true reality. Remember, just because you believe it, doesn't mean it's true.

_____

_____

_____

_____

_____

_____

_____

_____

_____

_____

_____

Matthew 6:22-23

[22] *"The eye is the lamp of the body. If your eyes are healthy,*[a]
your whole body will be full of light. [23] *But if your eyes are unhealthy,*[b]
your whole body will be full of darkness. If then the light within
you is darkness, how great is that darkness!

Do It for YOU Today!

When no one is looking, do the right thing. When no one is looking, go the extra mile. When no one is looking, do the last set of push-ups. When no else is looking put in the time, effort, and energy even if you'll never be noticed. Do it for you, do it for me, and do it because you're worth it and so are the people around you. The applause of man is fleeting but personal satisfaction and achievement carries with it an inner strength and confidence, which grows you into the person you long to be. Do that extra "something" today, especially when no one else is looking.

_____
_____
_____
_____
_____
_____
_____
_____
_____
_____
_____

James 2:18

18 But someone will say, "You have faith; I have deeds."
Show me your faith without deeds, and I will show you my
faith by my deeds.

Let Your Thoughts Be

Whose voice are you tuning into? Whose sound are you paying attention to? What words are you allowing to run through your mind? These are the game changers. The choices, which actually determine how your day goes. It's up to you to decide if you'll give into to fear, doubt, and worry or if you'll rise up and believe the absolute best about others and the situations around you. Start small, with one encouraging and motivating thought and slowly allow others to trickle in. These thoughts are your game changers – it's up to you to decide what you'll believe.

_____

_____

_____

_____

_____

_____

_____

_____

_____

_____

_____

_____

_____

John 6:35

³⁵ *Then Jesus declared, "I am the bread of life. Whoever comes to me will never go hungry, and whoever believes in me will never be thirsty.*

It's the Moments which You Create Your Life.

What are you choosing to do each and every day? It's your daily routine, which in fact creates for you the whole of your life. It's the little things that over time really do become the big things. Tasks, people, your to do list – everything adds up moment by moment and day by day. These rhythms you engage in become your normal, and often times that is good, very good, but sometimes it's not so good. It's important to take a step back, analyze your daily habits and ask yourself if this is the life you're longing to build?

_____

_____

_____

_____

_____

_____

_____

_____

_____

James 1:5-6

[5] *If any of you lacks wisdom, you should ask God, who gives generously to all without finding fault, and it will be given to you.* [6] *But when you ask, you must believe and not doubt, because the one who doubts is like a wave of the sea, blown and tossed by the wind.*

When Your Mind is at Rest, I'll Give You the Best.

Be on the look out for what I speak to you in the night. I come to you in your dreams, longing to give you sweet morsels of wisdom and to brighten your night with the trappings of my goodness. Sometimes these dreams won't make sense, but ask me, search me, and I'll show you the hidden treasures within. When your mind is at rest, I'll give you the best. Sweet dreams my friend for there is much I want to tell you.

_____

_____

_____

_____

_____

_____

_____

_____

_____

Psalm 16:6-8
⁶ The boundary lines have fallen for me in pleasant places;
surely, I have a delightful inheritance.
⁷ I will praise the LORD, who counsels me;
even at night my heart instructs me.
⁸ I keep my eyes always on the LORD.
With him at my right hand, I will not be shaken.

Build Yourself Up!

Build yourself up, build yourself up, and build yourself up. Again, and again when the world doesn't make sense, and anger seems to fill your every emotion, build yourself up. When all you want to do is scream, build yourself up. When chaos is all around you and it seems, no one is on your team, build yourself up. Learn to strengthen your heart, soul, and mind and dig into the hard work. Build yourself up and believe the best – it's a muscle you must strengthen each and every day.

_____

_____

_____

_____

_____

_____

_____

_____

_____

_____

_____

_____

_____

Hebrews 3:4

*⁴ For every house is built by someone,
but God is the builder of everything.*

Today will be a Good Day!

A good day is what you make of it. When you believe it will be good, when you move forward in faith, hope and love expecting a good day will be the outcome. When you have more mornings operating with great expectation, you'll have more evenings filled with deep peace. Don't forget a good day is unique to you and looks different for everyone. This day, TODAY, is *your good day*. Believe it, walk in it, shout it out, and keep your focus on me – THE one whose very nature is good. As I show you my goodness, *your good day* will take care of itself.

Psalm 107:1
¹ Give thanks to the LORD, for he is good;
his love endures forever.

I Give You Permission to Mix It Up Today!

Everyday you jump into your routine – your way of doing things that have become your normal. Today I am asking you to mix it up and step out of your everyday rhythm. I have new things to show you, new ways of doing things that will bring you added joy, delight and excitement. Go on a morning stroll, grocery shop at the other store today, or make that phone call before your normal tasks. Just because you've always done it a certain way doesn't mean you must always do it that way. Mix it up today – I give you permission!

_____

_____

_____

_____

_____

_____

_____

_____

_____

_____

Psalm 119:36-37

*36 Turn my heart toward your statutes
and not toward selfish gain.
37 Turn my eyes away from worthless things;
preserve my life according to your word.*[a]

Don't Delay – JUST DO IT!

If there's something good you know you must do, do it. Don't delay, don't hesitate, and don't hold back in any way, shape or form. Just do it. There's power in immediate action and following my voice quickly. It may seem silly, trite, or mediocre but as you know it's often the little things, the small acts of kindnesses, which carry the most weight and impact. Don't disregard those tugs of the spirit today, no matter how small or insignificant they may seem. Simply – just do it!

_____

_____

_____

_____

_____

_____

_____

_____

Deuteronomy 8:2-3
*² Remember how the LORD your God led you all the way
in the wilderness these forty years, to humble and test you in order to
know what was in your heart, whether or not you would keep
his commands. ³ He humbled you, causing you to hunger and
then feeding you with manna, which neither you nor your ancestors
had known, to teach you that man does not live on bread alone
but on every word that comes from the mouth of the LORD.*

Own What's Yours & See the Change.

I am asking you today to truly own what's yours. To take full responsibility for all that's in front of you and all who's around you - to push past your feelings and put other opinions aside and proceed. It will take discipline and self-control to create the life you dream about and the daily lifestyle you long to have. I am telling you today, you have what it takes to make these goals a reality. Keep going, keep fighting, and keep pushing. It will be worth it. I promise you that. Fully own what's your today and you won't regret it!

Ecclesiastes 11:6
6 Sow your seed in the morning,
and at evening let your hands not be idle,
for you do not know which will succeed,
whether this or that,
or whether both will do equally well.

I AM Waking You Up Today.

I am waking you up today. Calling you afresh to the sights, sounds, and senses of the day. I work where you might not have guessed. I show up where you least expect it. There's nothing I miss throughout the day. As the sun comes up and gives light to the earth, so am I causing you to rise up today and give light all around you. It's not a command that you must perform. It's just the true nature of who I have made you to be. So remember I am waking you up today with the goal to just be you!

_____
_____
_____
_____
_____
_____
_____
_____
_____
_____
_____
_____

Psalm 119:105
[105] *Your word is a lamp for my feet,*
a light on my path.

Though it Cost You All You Have Get Wisdom.

Though it may cost you much get wisdom, get understanding, and get insight. Let them be the guide for your actions keeping you steady on the path forward. So often we take for granted the little truths, which are actually the big truths, which keep us grounded and focused. You'll know what's good and wise by the fruit it bears. With every decision in front of you there's wisdom before it, calling you forth and showing you the way to go. Though it may cost you much, seek out this wisdom and let it be your guide. It will never steer you wrong.

Proverbs 16:16

*16 How much better to get wisdom than gold,
to get insight rather than silver!*

I Have Made You for the Spaces.

I am opening the doors of opportunity. It's time to advance, time to move forward with great anticipation and excitement. No more holding back, no more clinging to what's familiar or comfortable. I've made you for the spaces. I made you strong yet nimble, able to be flexible with every obstacle that comes your way. No more looking back on what was, only forward to the wide-open spaces in front of you. It's time to spread your wings and fly!

_____

_____

_____

_____

_____

_____

_____

_____

_____

_____

Isaiah 54:2

2 *"Enlarge the place of your tent,*
stretch your tent curtains wide,
do not hold back;
lengthen your cords,
strengthen your stakes.

The Power Lies in Your Focus.

There is power in focus. There is power in aligning your heart, soul and mind to one thing and one purpose. To tune in, dial in, and lock in to the goal in front of you not letting distractions get in the way of what you know you must do. It takes determination, will power, and pure endurance to keep your attention solely on the vision in front of you. Many opportunities will come your way, and lots of people with good intentions will offer you solutions, but you must decide this day and each day after where your focus will lie and to who and what will get your attention. The power lies in your focus.

_____

_____

_____

_____

_____

_____

_____

_____

_____

_____

_____

_____

_____

Philippians 4:13
13 I can do all this through him who gives me strength.

Be Devoted – with One Heart, Soul, and Mind.

Devotion these days seem to be a forgotten word. Something seen only in the movies and for the great athletes of our day. Yet I have called you to be devoted – with one heart, soul, and mind. There are the commitments I've placed before you, not heavy or burdensome, but light with my assistance. It's a daily decision you must make to be fully "all in" with your time, talents, and treasures. It won't be easy, it won't always be fun, but it will always be worth it. So what will you be fully devoted to this day and each day after?

_____

_____

_____

_____

_____

_____

_____

_____

_____

_____

_____

Deuteronomy 8:11

_¹¹ Be careful that you do not forget the LORD your God,
failing to observe his commands, his laws
and his decrees that I am giving you this day._

Walk with Me Today.

Take a walk with me today; a slow, steady, and peaceful walk. Here I'll give you clarity, here I'll give you wisdom, and here I'll show you your true reality. Get away from the noise, get away from the chaos, and step out of the rat race. I know there are things, which are heavy on your heart, problems you aren't sure how to solve, and an overwhelming sense that all the plates are about to fall. So walk with me this day and step-by-step I'll lighten your load and give you what you need so your steps are light and your bounce is joyful.

_____

_____

_____

_____

_____

_____

_____

_____

_____

_____

_____

_____

Exodus 33:14

*14 The LORD replied, "My Presence will go with you,
and I will give you rest."*

Ask Boldly, Seek Diligently, and Knock on the Door!

Ask, seek, and knock. Ask, seek, and knock and the door will be open. Are you asking? Are you seeking? Are you knocking? Each word implies an action. An opening of your mouth to let your voice be heard. Getting out of your chair to find what you're looking for. Move your hands to proactively pursue what's in front of you. Ask, seek, and knock is not just a catchy phrase I've given to you. It's a truth, and a promise that when you walk it out, you'll see your desires come to pass. So, ask, seek, and knock today – these are your action steps today!

_____

_____

_____

_____

_____

_____

_____

_____

_____

_____

_____

_____

Colossians 4:2

² *Devote yourselves to prayer, being watchful and thankful.*

Preparation Precedes Opportunity.

Remember preparation precedes opportunity. Before "your opportunity" arrives, it requires a diligent focus to prepare yourself for the main event. In the weeks of preparation, you are operating in pure faith trusting that all your hard work and commitment is not in vain but in fact is getting you ready for what you long to see manifest. These actions of faith and decisions of hope will be rewarded as the opportunity will show up right on time, right when you're ready. You can trust me on this!

_____

_____

_____

_____

_____

_____

_____

_____

_____

_____

_____

_____

_____

Deuteronomy 8:18
*18 But remember the LORD your God, for it is he who gives
you the ability to produce wealth, and so confirms his covenant,
which he swore to your ancestors, as it is today.*

Pick Just One Thing!

Pick one thing – just one area where you hear me talking and tune your attention to it. Narrow in on it, study it, and connect with me on it. Let's dive in deep together and watch how it helps answer all those other questions, doubts, and worries you have brewing at the surface. Disregard the other distractions and stay steadfast on this one thing. It will bring life, joy, and give you greater clarity. Don't spend too much time deciding what your one thing is. Go with your gut and pick the area I seem to be highlighting, then run with it!

_____

_____

_____

_____

_____

_____

_____

_____

_____

_____

_____

_____

_____

Luke 10:19

¹⁹ I have given you authority to trample on snakes and scorpions and to overcome all the power of the enemy; nothing will harm you.

One By One We Tackle Your Day.

I know you have a lot of moving parts in your life right now. Juggling task upon task and having to attend to what seems to be like an endless array of gatherings. Each moving piece is where I long to move and speak, showing you how I connect the dots and masterfully work it all together. As you move forward, I'll show you what to drop, what to lay aside for now, and where to run full speed ahead. Don't give up on all your moving parts instead let me guide you carefully, steadily one by one as we tackle them together!

_____

_____

_____

_____

_____

_____

_____

_____

_____

_____

_____

_____

_____

Psalm 31:24

²⁴ *Be strong and take heart,*
all you who hope in the LORD.

At Just the Right Time the Path will Light.

Let me be your teacher today, directing you and instructing you in the way you should go. I don't command orders telling you exactly what to do and when to do like a drill sergeant in the army. You're already on the journey and already searching for the piece of wisdom you need. As your teacher I turn the light on right when you need it, so your solution will appear right on time. Don't stand still in your tracks today but keep walking forward knowing clarity will come at the perfect time.

_____
_____
_____
_____
_____
_____
_____
_____
_____
_____
_____
_____
_____

Matthew 11:30

[30] *For my yoke is easy and my burden is light.*

Because There's Greatness Within You.

I see you stepping out. I see your taking strides towards the unknown, leaps of faith towards what could be, and jumping all in to the new season that's upon you. Even in your fear, doubt and worry you are moving forward, and I could not be prouder of you. You're pushing anxiety to the side, letting go of disappointment, and proving to yourself that you have what it takes. I know you've always had it in you, but I am happy to see you believe in YOU now too. Keep believing, my friend, because there's greatness within you. True greatness.

_____

_____

_____

_____

_____

_____

_____

Psalm 46:1-3

¹ God is our refuge and strength,
an ever-present help in trouble.
² Therefore we will not fear, though the earth give way
and the mountains fall into the heart of the sea,
³ though its waters roar and foam
and the mountains quake with their surging.[c]

Just Follow the One Voice!

Sometimes in life you must cut out the noise, cut out the fluff, cut out the other voices and tune into what's true. A sharp narrowing, and a focus that cuts through the junk. No more clutter, no more white noise, no more chaos and no more confusion. Just the one voice. It's life, it's breath, and energy to your soul. Don't allow anyone or anything to take it from you. Tune into it and tune out the rest. One voice and the rest will take care of itself. Your day just got a lot easier with only one voice to follow!

_____
_____
_____
_____
_____
_____
_____
_____
_____
_____
_____
_____
_____

Romans 8:37

[37] *No, in all these things we are more than conquerors through him who loved us.*

May
Devotional

Every Day I am Aligning You!

Everyday I am aligning you - your words, your actions, and your connections. I am putting the right people in your path, placing you in the proper positions, and setting up your circumstances so you don't miss a beat. It might not always look perfect and sometimes it may be downright messy but stay close to me and listen to my still small voice. Look for my alignment; look for where I am directing you and to whom I am directing you to. You might be surprised where I take you!

John 16:13

13 But when he, the Spirit of truth, comes, he will guide you into all the truth. He will not speak on his own; he will speak only what he hears, and he will tell you what is yet to come.

It's Time to Run with All Your Heart.

Run, my friend, run. Run towards your destiny. Run towards your goal. Run towards the vision in front of you and keep running. Be like Forrest Gump today – if he was going somewhere, he was runnnning! Move your arms with force, move your legs with determination and sprint towards the finish line. There are times when I call you to rest – to catch your breath and relax, but now I've called you to run. To embrace where you are and embrace what's around you with your eyes locked on the target and your focus straight ahead. It's time to run with all your heart in the direction of your dreams!

_____

_____

_____

_____

_____

_____

_____

_____

_____

_____

1 Timothy 6:11
¹¹But you, man of God, flee from all this, and pursue
righteousness, godliness, faith, love, endurance and gentleness.

Let "It" Go. "It's" Only Holding You Back."

Let it go! What people think does not define you. Let it go. You can't please everyone. Let it go! The opinions of others is not the voice you should listen to. Let it go! Holding onto previous hurts and offenses, you're only hurting yourself. Let it go! Past disappointments are now your rearview mirror and I am pointing you forward. Let it go! No more believing the lies in your head. Let it go, you are more than meets the eye. Let it go! It won't matter a year from now. Let *it* go because it's time for *you* to *go* forward!

Ephesians 6:13

[13] *Therefore put on the full armor of God,*
so that when the day of evil comes, you may be able to stand
your ground, and after you have done everything, to stand.

Letting Waiting Be Your Joy.

Sometimes waiting is the hardest - the part which seems to take the most time, energy and resources. Sitting, standing, preparing, and sitting some more – somehow it can suck the life out of you and when the time comes to move forward you find yourself wanting to stay put and sit longer. But this time as you wait, get up, and be proactive. Prepare and practice for the opportunity which awaits you. Ask me for a waiting plan so you don't become stagnant and complacent. Soon your waiting will become an absolute joy!

_____

_____

_____

_____

_____

_____

_____

_____

_____

_____

_____

_____

Colossians 3:12

¹² *Therefore, as God's chosen people, holy and dearly loved, clothe your-selves with compassion, kindness, humility, gentleness and patience.*

Wake Up Sleepy Head – I Have Blessing Waiting for You!

Wake up sleepy head. No more rolling over to hit snooze one more time. It's time to wake up. It's a fresh start to the day. Decide, that it will be great and worth getting out of bed. You can do it. You can commit to the goodness of the day and find yourself happy again. I have blessings waiting for you, opportunities at your door, and divine appointments ready for you. BUT it requires you to wake up, to wipe the sleep from your eyes and engage once again. You've done it before and now it's time to do it again. Wake up sleepy head!

_____

_____

_____

_____

_____

_____

_____

_____

_____

Psalm 119:1-2

¹ Blessed are those whose ways are blameless,
who walk according to the law of the LORD.
² Blessed are those who keep his statutes
and seek him with all their heart —

Put on Your Oxygen Mask First.

You can't be all things to everyone. It's not your job to make sure everyone is happy and always has what they need. Your job is to manage you - to tune into me and follow my voice each day. In doing so, you'll know where to be, who to help, and what tasks you can commit to. You won't always get it right and that's ok – it will have to be ok. Manage you – your emotions, your thoughts, and your behavior and at the end of the day if you're taking care of you, then the rest will take care of it itself.

_____

_____

_____

_____

_____

_____

_____

_____

_____

_____

Psalm 19:7

⁷ The law of the LORD is perfect,
refreshing the soul.
The statutes of the LORD are trustworthy,
making wise the simple.

Get Ready for the Breakthrough!

The sun is rising. The light is beginning to shine through. That alarm, that bell, and that release is coming. It's not a notification of danger or chaos but instead an alert to say, "Hey, now's the time." While you've been waiting, He's been preparing you step-by-step, for such a time as this. Get ready to be launched forward for the sun is rising. The day is new – get ready for the breakthrough!

_____

_____

_____

_____

_____

_____

_____

_____

_____

_____

_____

_____

_____

_____

Psalm 119:114

[114] *You are my refuge and my shield;*
I have put my hope in your word.

Let Me Shift Your Perspective Today!

Every misstep, every mistake, every wrong turn can be fixed. In a moment I can swoop in and turn the tide, and turn the table towards your good, towards your advancement. Each time when you think you've failed is an opportunity to learn, grow, and do things differently. These instances don't define you, but you should allow them to shape you and mold you and craft you for the purpose before you. A failure in your eyes may be a true victory in my eyes. Let me shift your perspective today and show you what I see.

_____

_____

_____

_____

_____

_____

_____

_____

Isaiah 55:8-9

8 *"For my thoughts are not your thoughts,*
neither are your ways my ways,"
declares the LORD.
9 *"As the heavens are higher than the earth,*
so are my ways higher than your ways
and my thoughts than your thoughts.

I Have More Than Enough Time for You.

There's no need to rush, no need to worry, no need to doubt what's ahead. I go before you. I can see the future and it looks bright. I live before time, within time, and outside of time and can help you manage your time. It may feel as if there aren't enough hours in the day but I know just what you need to accomplish during every waking minute and will help you master it all. There's no need to rush, no need to worry, and no need to doubt – I am helping you get everything done and there's just enough time for you to get it all done!

Psalm 72:12

[12] *For he will deliver the needy who cry out,*
the afflicted who have no one to help.

I Give You the Space You Need Today.

Today my friend, I am letting you know you have space. Space to talk, space to vent, space to voice your opinions, space to express your anger, hurt, and frustration, and space to breathe. I am here ready to listen, ready to sit with you in it all, and give you the space you need to keep going. You may not feel like you have the space with those around you, but with me you get to speak what's on your mind. So tell me it all today. Whisper, shout, and declare it in my ear. I am here, I am listening, and I am giving you the space you need today.

_____

_____

_____

_____

_____

_____

_____

_____

Psalm 91:9-11

⁹ If you say, "The Lord is my refuge,"
and you make the Most High your dwelling,
¹⁰ no harm will overtake you,
no disaster will come near your tent.
¹¹ For he will command his angels concerning you
to guard you in all your ways;

From the Inside Out, I am Healing You.

From the inside out, I am healing you. Taking care of your heart, mind, body and soul. The world looks at the symptoms and the behavior and tries to diagnose and put a Band-Aid on what seems wrong. I do the opposite, as I do a deep dive into the very heart of the matter, addressing the "weed" and fully getting rid of that nasty root in your life. No more skirting around the issue, no more sugar coating the problem, I have come to give you true life and it starts from deep within. Let me dig deep today and fully heal you – inside AND out.

_____

_____

_____

_____

_____

_____

_____

_____

_____

_____

_____

Matthew 14:28

[28] *"Lord, if it's you," Peter replied,*
"tell me to come to you on the water."

No More Numbing, My Friend.

*N*umb - *to totally cut off all feeling, all sensation, and all sense of emotion in order to block out and completely ignore what's really going on beneath the surface.* Remember I haven't called you to numb away your pain, anger, or hurt. I haven't asked to set aside your disappointment, frustration and annoyances. I haven't asked you to hide your feelings and *just get on with it.* Embrace where you're at, dive into what's beneath the surface, and address what's really going on. If you'll be honest I'll meet you there and help move you forward. No more numbing my friend!

Isaiah 12:2

²*Surely God is my salvation;*
I will trust and not be afraid.
The LORD, the LORD himself, is my strength and my defense[a];
he has become my salvation."

You're Building Strength from the Inside Out.

Y ou're gaining strength, endurance, and stamina. With each step it may seem like it could be your last, but in fact you're building critical muscle. From the inside out, I am building an inner resolve which will stand the storms. These inner muscles are what sustains you and keeps you going. You can't see it, others can't see it, but soon you'll look back and see yourself getting stronger. Your inside transformation will be evident from your outside actions. With every step remember your true reality – you're building strength from the inside out!

Nehemiah 8:10

¹⁰ *Nehemiah said, "Go and enjoy choice food and sweet drinks, and send some to those who have nothing prepared. This day is holy to our Lord. Do not grieve, for the joy of the LORD is your strength."*

I Believe in You. I Believe in You. I Believe in You.

I believe you. I believe your words, your actions, and your behavior. I believe you. When the world and others don't seem to trust you or seem to believe what you have to say. I believe you. I see you and hear all you have to say. Even the words you don't express, I hear those as well and feel your every emotion. I believe you today and trust you fully. Stand tall today even when others make you feel two feet tall. You have much to be proud of and much to say. I believe you and most importantly I believe *in you*.

_____

_____

_____

_____

_____

_____

_____

_____

_____

_____

Psalm 23:5

5 You prepare a table before me
in the presence of my enemies.
You anoint my head with oil;
my cup overflows.

Remember, It's Me Who Gives Life.

At the end of the day when all seems lost and it takes all your energy just to crawl into bed, remember I give you all you need. At the end of the day, when you can't engage in another call, text or piece of information, remember I fill you up. At the end of the day, when you're out of toothpaste and you want to scream at the world, remember I provide your every need. At the end of the day, when you remember you have a 7:00am meeting, don't forget I sustain you. At the end of the day when it seems like know one has noticed you, remember I see you. Above all, at the end of the day, when no one is around, remember I love you!

_____

_____

_____

_____

_____

_____

_____

_____

_____

_____

Psalm 17:8

8 Keep me as the apple of your eye;
hide me in the shadow of your wings

147

Rest, Rest, Rest – Truly Rest Today.

Learn how to rest. The world will tell you to veg out, binge on a Netflix, go out on the town, and completely forget about the day's troubles - only to wake up not having rested at all and once again finding yourself right where you left off. When you "check out" nothing is ever gained. Seek today to find true rest, and engage in those activities that give you life and surround yourself with those people who build you up. Learn to rest today so you'll be recharged tomorrow!

_____

_____

_____

_____

_____

_____

_____

_____

_____

_____

_____

Hebrews 4:9-11
9 There remains, then, a Sabbath-rest for the people of God;
10 for anyone who enters God's rest also rests from their works,[a] just as God did from his. 11 Let us, therefore, make every effort to enter that rest, so that no one will perish by following their example of disobedience.

I Trust You with It All.

I trust you with the big things and the little things and everything in between. There's a strength within you that grows each day. A strength, which displays your integrity, honesty, and humility, and allows me to trust you. In your integrity I see a grace arising, in your honestly I see a warrior arising, and in your humility I see a leader arising. Look around and see all the people and tasks I've entrusted you with – the big, the little and everything in between. Always remember, I trust you, so *you* can trust in you!

_____

_____

_____

_____

_____

_____

_____

_____

_____

_____

_____

Psalm 91:1-2
[1] *Whoever dwells in the shelter of the Most High*
will rest in the shadow of the Almighty.[a]
[2] *I will say of the LORD, "He is my refuge and my fortress,*
my God, in whom I trust."

149

I Believe in You – Without a Doubt in My Mind.

Without a doubt I believe in you – in the person you're becoming. I believe in you – without a doubt. There's no hesitation in my mind, no worry or wonder if you have what it takes. I know and each day I long to affirm this truth in you. Appointments are coming, and opportunities are on there way – all because I believe in you. No more waiting, no more hiding, no more beating around the bush. I believe in you today – in all that you are and all you are doing.

_____

_____

_____

_____

_____

_____

_____

_____

_____

_____

Genesis 12:2
2 *"I will make you into a great nation,*
and I will bless you;
I will make your name great,
and you will be a blessing.[a]

Cut Out the Unnecessary so the Necessary can Speak!

Simplify today. Remove the clutter, noise and chaos which blot out your peace, joy and love. Cut out the unnecessary so that the necessary can speak. Dial back on your to do list so what's most important gets done. Stop the rat race and let your heart find peace once again. It's time to simplify today – to make what seems hard and complicated incredibly easy. Keep your list small, let your calendar have white space and watch to see how I move when nothing else unnecessary gets in the way!

_____

_____

_____

_____

_____

_____

_____

_____

_____

_____

_____

_____

_____

Isaiah 55:6

[6] *Seek the LORD while he may be found;*
call on him while he is near.

Guard Your Heart, for from it Flows Life!

If your heart is a container, what are you filling it with? Love, peace, joy and faith? Or pain, discouragement, frustration or fear? Your heart is where I live and where life flows out. Guard it like your life depends on it because it does. Remember to fill it regularly, keep it hydrated with joy, keep it saturated with peace, and keep it overflowing with love - making sure only the best enters in. Take ownership of the heart I've given you. It's your container – guard it with your life, because remember…your LIFE depends on it!

_____

_____

_____

_____

_____

_____

_____

_____

_____

_____

_____

Proverbs 4:23

²³ *Above all else, guard your heart,*
for everything you do flows from it.

Pace Yourself Today.

Pace yourself. Life isn't a sprint to see who can get the most done. Life isn't a test to see if you have what it takes. Life isn't a job where you must work yourself to death. So pace yourself today and find a rhythm, which is sustainable, which is steady and keeps your energy always flowing. Choose routines that work with you and for you, rather than against you. You're not on the rat race of life – you're on the track of abundance and peace. Pace yourself today – there's more life to be lived and I want you at your best each step of the way!

_____

_____

_____

_____

_____

_____

_____

_____

Proverbs 30:7-8

7 *"Two things I ask of you, Lord;*
do not refuse me before I die:
8 *Keep falsehood and lies far from me;*
give me neither poverty nor riches,
but give me only my daily bread.

Start to Expect the Unexpected.

It's time to hope again. To believe again that your dreams, goals, and desires will come to life. Let go of disappointment, put aside those feelings of complete despair, and grab a seed of faith once again. Imagine yourself planting it in the ground and each day you water it, care for it, and tend it – finding it in your heart to trust again that *"it"* will come to pass, and my perfect timing is just around the corner. Build up your confidence and expect the unexpected. It's time to start fighting again and know that something better and greater is *surely* yet to come!

Psalm 84:4

⁴ Blessed are those who dwell in your house;
they are ever praising you.[a]

154

They Need You and You Need Them – Find Your Army.

Draw an army around you. A group of people you can rely on, depend on, and lean on. They need you and you need them. Don't get cozy on your comfortable island as you isolate yourself from the world because I've built you for relationships and I've created you for community. You can't get to where you want to go without these divinely placed relationships I have for you. Discern the season you're in, and take note of who I am placing in your path. Some people may be for a short time, and others longer but the same rule applies – they need you and you need them. Find your army.

_____

_____

_____

_____

_____

_____

_____

James 4:11-12

[11] *Brothers and sisters, do not slander one another. Anyone who speaks against a brother or sister[a] or judges them speaks against the law and judges it. When you judge the law, you are not keeping it, but sitting in judgment on it.* [12] *There is only one Lawgiver and Judge, the one who is able to save and destroy. But you — who are you to judge your neighbor?*

Just Take a Second – to Catch Your Breath.

Just hang out with me for a second. Give me a moment to speak, to breathe, to calm your weary mind, and take a load off. Find me in this moment. Here, I am talking and you're listening and you're talking, and I am listening. Back and forth and back and forth we go until you find your breath again and clarity starts to take shape. Just a moment is all I need and you'll find you will leave with much more than you came with.

_____

_____

_____

_____

_____

_____

_____

_____

_____

_____

_____

_____

Ezekiel 11:19

[19] *I will give them an undivided heart and put a new spirit in them; I will remove from them their heart of stone and give them a heart of flesh.*

156

Take Time to Consider
Who I am Considering.

Take time to consider whom I am considering. All day long you're surrounded by tasks, dishes, appointments, laundry, and people vying for your attention – pause for a second and ask me who's on my heart. There's someone I want to highlight, someone who needs a word, someone who needs to know that someone cares and will appreciate the time you took to reach out. Get out from your world, get out from the rat race to listen to who "that person" is. When you do, you'll see it's truly better to give than receive.

_____

_____

_____

_____

_____

_____

_____

_____

_____

_____

Mark 1:16-17
*16 As Jesus walked beside the Sea of Galilee, he saw
Simon and his brother Andrew casting a net into the lake,
for they were fishermen. 17 "Come, follow me," Jesus said,
"and I will send you out to fish for people."*

You're More Important than any Task in Front of You!

Y ou are more important than any task you get done. Your health, your well-being, your mental state of mind is more important than checking off another box on your to do list. Know your limits, know what extra activity would put you over the edge and know how to say no when you've been pushed too far. Taking time for you is what allows you to keep moving forward and gives people the best of you. Rest is in your DNA and it's needed – never forget you're more important than any task in front of you!

_____

_____

_____

_____

_____

_____

_____

_____

_____

Psalm 84:11

¹¹ For the LORD God is a sun and shield;
the LORD bestows favor and honor;
no good thing does he withhold
from those whose walk is blameless.

Be a Starter Today.

Be a starter. Someone who takes intuitive, decides to call forth action, and rallies a team forward. Decide today to begin for the first time or maybe again for the 50th time to be a starter. Don't wait, being dependent on other people to make things happen – charge forward and get the ball rolling. Plow ahead today and take action on what I've called you towards. You have what you need, you have what it takes, and no one is holding you back. Be a starter today!

_____

_____

_____

_____

_____

_____

_____

_____

_____

_____

_____

_____

_____

Psalm 118:14

[14] *The LORD is my strength and my defense[a];*
he has become my salvation.

Be a Finisher.

Be a finisher. Be the one who completes what they started and makes it a point to fully see a project through. Be the person who understands it takes time, energy, tenacity, determination, and perseverance to walk something out to the very end. Endure today and fight hard to keep going with what needs to get done. There's a finish line and you can see it and you have what it takes to get there. Don't give up. I promise you a reward is waiting for you on the other side. The victory is yours. Keep going today and be a finisher till the end!

_____
_____
_____
_____
_____
_____
_____
_____
_____
_____
_____

2 Timothy 3:16-17
[16] *All Scripture is God-breathed and is useful for teaching, rebuking, correcting and training in righteousness,* [17] *so that the servant of God[a] may be thoroughly equipped for every good work.*

I am Giving You New Normals!

I am giving you new normals, new routines, and new ways of doing things which may feel awkward, weird, and out of place but stick with them and soon you'll find your new normal will become comfortable, easy, and take you to the next level. Lean into the chaos, lean into your new schedule, and lean into the abnormal and in no time, you'll be operating with great ease and loving your new rhythm. Stay the course today as what is now uncomfortable will soon become comfortable!

_____

_____

_____

_____

_____

_____

_____

_____

_____

_____

_____

_____

_____

Job 23:14
¹⁴ He carries out his decree against me,
and many such plans he still has in store.

Ask Me Today for that One Ingredient.

Sometimes it only takes one missing ingredient to ruin a whole batch of cookies. That one ingredient is needed and necessary for the perfect outcome. Ask me today for the one ingredient you might be missing. Seek me today for the one ingredient that will allow your days to flow more smoothly. Knock on my door today and see how I will give you that one thing you may not even realize you need. Ask, seek, and knock and watch how I divinely place it in your lap.

_____

_____

_____

_____

_____

_____

_____

_____

_____

_____

_____

_____

_____

_____

Jeremiah 33:3

[3] *'Call to me and I will answer you and tell you great and unsearchable things you do not know.'*

Look at Me Today – Only Me.

Y ou need moments when you don't look at your calendar, don't look at your to do list, and only look at me. Times in the day when you allow me to give you your marching orders, set your day and your agenda. These are the times I can breathe into your life, give you clarity, show you your true reality, and open up your eyes and ears to a new perspective. Put aside your planner, put aside your everyday routine and move forward with the sound of my voice. It's the only direction you need today.

_____

_____

_____

_____

_____

_____

_____

_____

_____

_____

_____

_____

_____

Psalm 46:1

¹ God is our refuge and strength,
an ever-present help in trouble.

June
Devotional

Don't Despise Your Small Beginnings.

The little things are just as important as the big things and sometimes even more important. The little acts of kindness you do, and the little tasks you finish throughout the day. All these little things are adding up to become the big things. It's the little things that often determine when you can step into the bigger arena. Don't dismiss your seemingly small commitments today as they are the very things which are getting you to where you want to go.

_____

_____

_____

_____

_____

_____

_____

_____

_____

_____

Proverbs 3:1-2
[1] My son, do not forget my teaching,
but keep my commands in your heart,
[2] for they will prolong your life many years
and bring you peace and prosperity.

The Important Things in Life Take Time.

The important things in life take time, like relationships, job satisfaction, trust, health, and love. They all require a commitment and a decision, which you need to make each and every day. This daily pursuit over time is where you will see change. It's where growth starts to occur, and you understand what's truly valuable. So, take time to invest today in these larger goals knowing you're in it for the long haul. The important things that really matter take time, and time is what I've given you.

_____

_____

_____

_____

_____

_____

_____

_____

_____

_____

Matthew 10:29-31

*29 Are not two sparrows sold for a penny? Yet not one of them
will fall to the ground outside your Father's care. 30 And even
the very hairs of your head are all numbered. 31 So don't be afraid;
you are worth more than many sparrows.*

You Have Just Enough Time.

Y ou have enough time - all the time in the world in fact. It may seem like time is pressed, and there aren't enough hours in the day, but everyday I appoint you the right amount of time you need to get everything done for the day. I know how long everything will take, I know what *actually* needs to be accomplished each day, so you can knock it out. No need to rush, hurry and frantically panic. Just remember what I have truly called you to do for this day and you'll see you have plenty of time.

_____

_____

_____

_____

_____

_____

_____

_____

_____

_____

Proverbs 4:1-2
¹ *Listen, my sons, to a father's instruction;*
pay attention and gain understanding.
² *I give you sound learning,*
so do not forsake my teaching.

169

You Have What You Need!

Yes, you have what need! Looking to the right, to the left, and at everyone around you is a recipe for disaster. In doing so, you'll quickly see what they have and think you're missing out, when in fact you have what you need for your specific needs. That is the TRUTH. You have been called for a specific and unique purpose, and I know what you need and when you need it. Move forward knowing I've placed all you require at your disposal and at the proper time you'll have everything that you need!

_____

_____

_____

_____

_____

_____

_____

_____

_____

_____

_____

_____

_____

Jeremiah 32:27

²⁷ *"I am the LORD, the God of all mankind.*
Is anything too hard for me?

Without a Doubt I am All You Need.

Without a doubt you can depend on me. Without a doubt you can trust in me. Without a doubt I have all you need, knowing I am paving the way. Without a doubt I am 100% on your side and giving you my very best. Without a doubt I am there when you need me. I see your every need, want, and desire. Without a doubt I have the solutions for your problems, and you can always depend on me. Without a doubt!

_____

_____

_____

_____

_____

_____

_____

_____

_____

_____

_____

_____

Isaiah 12:2
²Surely God is my salvation;
I will trust and not be afraid.
The LORD, the LORD himself, is my strength and my defense;
he has become my salvation."

A Bump in the Road is Just a Bump in the Road.

A bump in the road is merely a bump in the road. You decide how you'll react, how you'll respond, and if you'll let it keep you from moving forward. Eyes ahead and you'll learn to soar over those bumps. It's just a bump – not a deal breaker that will ruin your life. Just a hiccup and an unexpected turn of events in which you decide how you'll react going forward. Maybe you need to make an adjustment, maybe a slight change of pace, or maybe nothing changes at all. You have the wisdom; you have knowledge to decide and remember it's just a bump. Don't react like it's a wall.

---

2 Thessalonians 1:4

⁴ Therefore, among God's churches we boast about your perseverance and faith in all the persecutions and trials you are enduring.

Don't Forget to EnJOY the Ride!

Don't forget to enjoy the ride and enjoy the everyday adventure. No matter how mundane, routine, and normal your day may seem, make a point to find multiple pieces of happiness all throughout the day. You're not meant to merely go through the motions. You're not meant to mindlessly accomplish task after task, but rather go out and find joy in these little moments and find happiness in the small things. Joy is marked in your DNA so don't forget to enjoy the ride!

Galatians 5:22-23

²² But the fruit of the Spirit is love, joy, peace, forbearance, kindness, goodness, faithfulness, ²³ gentleness and self-control. Against such things there is no law.

Give Careful Thought to the Way You Should Go.

Give careful thought to the way you should go. Give careful consideration to the direction in front of you. Be mindful of the power of your choices. Be mindful of the opinions of others and the positive or negative effect they may have on you. Tread carefully today. Steadily move forward, conscious of each and every step. You have time to contemplate your path forward; you have time to prayerfully consider your way. No need to rush, hurry, and frantically blaze ahead. There's time for you today to carefully discern the next steps you must take and the direction you must go.

_____

_____

_____

_____

_____

_____

_____

_____

_____

_____

_____

_____

Proverbs 4:26

26 Give careful thought to the paths for your feet
and be steadfast in all your ways.

Jump in Today – ALL IN – with ALL you have!

Be all in today. All in with your time, your talents, your resources, your finances - commit them all to the direction you are going. Fully dive in, take the plunge and decide today that nothing will hold you back from moving forward. You have a destiny, a purpose, and a destination that's meant for you and you alone and I could not be prouder of the progress you have made. At the right time I'll accelerate you forward, so jump in today – ALL IN with ALL you have!

---

1 Timothy 4:15-16

[15] *Be diligent in these matters; give yourself wholly to them, so that everyone may see your progress.* [16] *Watch your life and doctrine closely. Persevere in them, because if you do, you will save both yourself and your hearers.*

Remove What's Toxic!

Move back from the people, and circumstances that prove toxic in your life. They serve no benefit to your well-being and are only dragging you down. Toxic thoughts, toxic behavior, toxic conversations, and toxic attitudes are hindering your ability to move forward and keep you from the change you want to see. They lock you up, tie you up, and keep you bound. Notice today what needs to go, who needs some distance, and where there's opportunity to free yourself from the toxic fumes. Soon you'll discover the freedom of purging all that's holding you back.

_____

_____

_____

_____

_____

_____

_____

Proverbs 26:20-22

[20] Without wood a fire goes out;
without a gossip a quarrel dies down.
[21] As charcoal to embers and as wood to fire,
so is a quarrelsome person for kindling strife.
[22] The words of a gossip are like choice morsels;
they go down to the inmost parts.

It's Time to Take Off!

It's time to take off. To fly, to soar and spread your wings. At first you may feel shaky, out of place, disoriented, and even a little confused, but remember you're in a new place, so give yourself time, grace, and patience to get comfortable with your new surroundings. You're right where you're supposed to be, and fulfilling your destiny, not missing a beat. Take time to examine what's around you, who's around you, and the FRESH season that's upon you. It may seem like you're a baby bird just learning to fly. Keep flapping your wings as it's time to take off!

_____

_____

_____

_____

_____

_____

_____

Isaiah 40:30-31

30 Even youths grow tired and weary,
and young men stumble and fall;
31 but those who hope in the LORD
will renew their strength.
They will soar on wings like eagles;
they will run and not grow weary,
they will walk and not be faint.

177

Be Thankful for How Far You've Come.

It's a cycle of waiting, preparing, waiting and preparing with more waiting and preparing, wondering if you will ever get to your desired destination. Yet each step is necessary in the process. Skipping one step potentially means your next step will be delayed. It's a process, a journey, and you can't forget that each step should be just as exciting as the "destination" you're shooting towards. Take notice of the cycle you are in and be thankful for how far you've come – it's a process with much to learn along the way!

_____

_____

_____

_____

_____

_____

_____

_____

_____

_____

_____

_____

_____

_____

Hebrews 6:15
15 And so after waiting patiently,
Abraham received what was promised.

Choose Today to Choose Joy!

Sometimes it's as simple as mere decision. To decide, to make up in your mind that life will be good, there is opportunity at your doorstep and there will be better days ahead. To decide to resolve your thinking that it's a new day, full of possibilities surrounded by those who truly care about you. To decide and choose to believe that you're in a season, and this too shall pass, and you will get through what's in front of you. Sometimes it's as simple as a mere decision and a simple matter of the mind!

_____

_____

_____

_____

_____

_____

_____

_____

_____

_____

_____

Deuteronomy 16:15
15 For seven days celebrate the festival to the LORD your God at the place the LORD will choose. For the LORD your God will bless you in all your harvest and in all the work of your hands, and your joy will be complete.

Check in with Me Today – I Long to Check in with You!

When seemingly no one has time for you, no one has a moment to check in and see how you are doing, remember I am always making time for you, space for you, and moments for you to check in with me. Let me know how you're doing, let me hear what's going on, and how I can help you this day. I care, I want to help, and I want to hear from you – now and always. I am making time for you, clearing my schedule to dial into your heart and mind today. You are on MY mind today and I consider you of utmost importance. Check in with me today because I am longing to check in with you!

_____

_____

_____

_____

_____

_____

_____

_____

_____

_____

Romans 6:11

11 *In the same way, count yourselves dead to sin but alive to God in Christ Jesus.*

State Your Needs Boldly Today!

It's ok to have needs. We all have them. They've been crafted into your DNA, into your wiring and into the heartbeat of who you are. These are the details of life that in fact give you life and keep you going. They are necessary to get you through each and every week. They are your breath when life's troubles choke the life out of you. Be bold to state your needs, what's important to you and necessary for your day-to-day survival. It's not selfish. It's showing your dependence on others and your need for each other and for me. Be honest with yourself and others about what you need – you're important and you're need is just as important as well!

_____

_____

_____

_____

_____

_____

Jeremiah 1:6-8
6 *"Alas, Sovereign LORD," I said, "I do not know
how to speak; I am too young."*
7 *But the LORD said to me, "Do not say, 'I am too young.' You must go to
everyone I send you to and say whatever I command you.*
8 *Do not be afraid of them, for I am with you and will rescue you,"
declares the LORD.*

You're Crossing Over – New Territory Ahead!

You're crossing over into new territory, a new domain, which has your name written all over it. So dive in and believe in yourself and believe in the gifts within you and the skills you've acquired. No more holding back. No more hanging onto holding patterns and old ways of thinking. Nothing can stop this transition. You're crossing over and it will be awkward and uncomfortable at first but let that be a confirmation that you're headed in the right direction and you're right where you're suppose to be!

_____

_____

_____

_____

_____

_____

Isaiah 54:4-5

⁴ *"Do not be afraid; you will not be put to shame.*
Do not fear disgrace; you will not be humiliated.
You will forget the shame of your youth
and remember no more the reproach of your widowhood.
⁵ *For your Maker is your husband —*
the LORD Almighty is his name —
the Holy One of Israel is your Redeemer;
he is called the God of all the earth.

STOP the Rat Race of Life.

Stop. Stop the rat race. Stop tackling your to do list. Stop ticking off boxes and feeling like you've accomplished and mastered the day. Stop mindlessly over working yourself and stop burning yourself out week in and week out. Stop even before you start, learn to first check in with me. Rush too much and you'll miss me, fly by the seat of your pants and you'll miss me, chase the storms of life and you'll miss me. Too much, too quickly and you'll miss me. Stop the rat race – it just might save your life.

_____

_____

_____

_____

_____

_____

_____

_____

_____

_____

Psalm 42:11

11 Why, my soul, are you downcast?
Why so disturbed within me?
Put your hope in God,
for I will yet praise him,
my Savior and my God.

Excellence is Who You Are!

Check and double check and check again because excellence is in your DNA. The jobs, the tasks, the people I have put into your life are given as a privilege, a gift for you to cherish. Check in on how they are doing, double check to see if you took care of every detail. Be faithful with what I place in your lap and whom I place around you. Be loyal, consistent, and careful to not overlook the significance they hold in your life. Mark your days, tasks, and appointments by excellence – for this is the standard I have set for you.

_____
_____
_____
_____
_____
_____
_____
_____
_____
_____
_____

1 Corinthians 2:16

"Who has known the mind of the Lord
so as to instruct him?"
But we have the mind of Christ.

Let Wisdom Guide You Today.

Let God's wisdom and guidance be your friend today. Your guide, your solution, and the one you seek when you want to throw your hands in the air and run the other direction. Let wisdom lead you towards peace, prosperity, and provision. Allow wisdom to have space in your heart and mind to speak to the problems that met you this morning. Without wisdom you won't know the way. Let wisdom be your friend today!

_____

_____

_____

_____

_____

_____

_____

_____

_____

_____

_____

_____

_____

_____

Proverbs 1:7
⁷ The fear of the LORD is the beginning of knowledge,
but fools despise wisdom and instruction.

Moment by Moment You're Creating Your Future.

Piece by piece, bit-by-bit, moment-by-moment and day-by-day you are creating the future in front of you. Your actions, your choices, and your behavior determine your success. Each decision may feel small, insignificant, and trivial even but over time these daily decisions layout your future pathway. So choose carefully and be mindful of your actions – understanding this is your life you're creating!

_____

_____

_____

_____

_____

_____

_____

_____

_____

_____

_____

Haggai 1:5
⁵ *Now this is what the LORD Almighty says:*
"Give careful thought to your ways.

Every Decision Costs You Something.

Sacrifice. Not the most popular word. Not the most appealing word. Not the most talked about word. Yet a word when applied to your life and applied to the right situations is the most rewarding of words. Everyday you make sacrifices because every decision costs you something. It may be your time, your money, or your resources. Today connect with me and make sure you're sacrificing for the right reasons and the right things. It can either be the most rewarding of words or the most depleting. Are your sacrifices for me or for yourself?

Proverbs 16:2

² All a person's ways seem pure to them,
but motives are weighed by the LORD.

The New Space is Meant Just for You!

The tension you feel is YOU being stretched, pressed on every side, and seemingly bent in every direction. This awkwardness, uneasiness, and unfamiliarity is getting you out of sorts. You might wonder what exactly is going on and if you're on the right track. Let me assure you this day that you are right where you need to be. These feelings are all confirmation that you are growing, maturing, and moving into new and fresh territory. Allow yourself to settle into what feels like foreign ground and spread your wings because this NEW SPACE is meant just for you!

_____

_____

_____

_____

_____

_____

_____

_____

_____

_____

_____

Luke 6:38

[38] *Give, and it will be given to you. A good measure, pressed down,*
shaken together and running over, will be poured into your lap.
For with the measure you use, it will be measured to you."

Let Your Focus Lead You Forward.

How would your life look different if your focus was locked in on what you truly desired? What would change? What would stay the same? How would your relationships look? How would your day-to-day activities change? All questions posed around a single word – focus. Focus is the central point which grabs your attention and determines your activity. So today seek to cut out distractions that steal your focus and say no to engagements that take your eye off the prize. Resolve today to let your FOCUS lead you FORWARD.

_____

_____

_____

_____

_____

_____

_____

_____

_____

_____

_____

_____

2 Chronicles 16:9

⁹ For the eyes of the LORD range throughout the earth to
strengthen those whose hearts are fully committed to him.
You have done a foolish thing, and from now on you will be at war."

Nothing Can Keep Me from You!

"There ain't no mountain high enough, and there ain't no valley low enough that can keep me getting from you." Catchy lyrics but none the less the truth which I sing over you each day. Nothing can keep me from you. No mind barrier or wrong action can hinder our connection. Absolutely nothing and NO ONE can keep me from pouring out my love to you and pursuing you with all that I am. It's who I am as a devoted Father and nothing will get in the way of my pursuit towards you.

_____

_____

_____

_____

_____

_____

_____

_____

_____

_____

_____

_____

_____

_____

Psalm 89:28

28 I will maintain my love to him forever,
and my covenant with him will never fail.

Ask Me Where to Unsubscribe Today!

Unsubscribe. It's placed strategically at the very bottom of each email in the smallest of fonts. Like a detective on the hunt, you must track that one word down. Maybe the emails aren't relevant, maybe they send way too many, or maybe you're just tired of a cluttered inbox. Whatever the reason, you've had enough. Unsubscribe. Your everyday life is no different. With a barrage of messages filling your mind it can quickly exceed capacity. Today ask me where you can "unsubscribe". Ask me where there's opportunity to hit delete and let me show you how to find more space in your "inbox"!

Psalm 42:1-2

¹ As the deer pants for streams of water,
so my soul pants for you, my God.
² My soul thirsts for God, for the living God.
When can I go and meet with God?

Don't Forget You're Part of a Family.

Don't forget you are part of a family. Not just your blood family but the wider family who've I purposed around you. Some people may come and go, and some relationships may just be for a season, but pay attention to whom I am sending you. Those people, those relationships, those friendships, and those bonds which cut through the junk, the crap, and build a foundation of trust. Lock arms with them this week. Commit to being in the thick of it with them. Be real, be raw, and be you when you are with them. They need you and you need them. It's what I've designed family to be all about.

_____

_____

_____

_____

_____

_____

_____

_____

_____

Proverbs 11:14

[14] *For lack of guidance a nation falls,*
but victory is won through many advisers.

Find Time to Cut Out the Noise Today!

Day in and day out it can get noisy – just plain loud, and it can be hard to discern your thoughts, your friend's thoughts, your family's thoughts from the Lord's thoughts. Lots of voices, lots of opinions, and lots of comments all resulting in lots of noise. You must find your quiet, find your "turn it down" button, and center in on my voice. My voice is calm, cool, and collected – no more chaos. Hearing me you'll find your peace, find your joy, and be brought back to the true reality in front of you. Find time to cut out the noise today and you'll be rewarded!

_____

_____

_____

_____

_____

_____

Isaiah 55:1-2

"Come, all you who are thirsty,
come to the waters;
and you who have no money,
come, buy and eat!
Come, buy wine and milk
without money and without cost.
² Why spend money on what is not bread,
and your labor on what does not satisfy?

How You Steward Today is How You'll Show Up Tomorrow.

Y ou have responsibilities and duties in your life which require your time, energy and attention. You have demands and commitments that have your name attached to them. I am calling you today to be a good steward to what and who is in front of you. Stay the course and stay committed to the tasks you have agreed to do and seek to do them with excellence. These seemingly everyday responsibilities are the avenue I use to launch you forward.

_____

_____

_____

_____

_____

_____

_____

_____

_____

_____

1 Corinthians 10:13

[13] No temptation has overtaken you except what is common to mankind. And God is faithful; he will not let you be tempted beyond what you can bear. But when you are tempted, he will also provide a way out so that you can endure it.

Say Yes to Living Outside the Box Today!

It's not about going through the motions, like a mindless, emotionless robot. I've created you for adventure, fun, and joy. You have my permission to mix it up today, think outside of the box and live outside of the box. Let different, new, and fresh be words that define you today. Get creative with all that's in front you. Your to do list doesn't rule your life. Say yes to tackling your day with a spirit of joy and adventure. Say no to the mundane routines of life.

_____

_____

_____

_____

_____

_____

_____

_____

_____

Judges 3:28-30

²⁸ *"Follow me," he ordered, "for the LORD has given Moab, your enemy, into your hands." So they followed him down and took possession of the fords of the Jordan that led to Moab; they allowed no one to cross over.* ²⁹ *At that time they struck down about ten thousand Moabites, all vigorous and strong; not one escaped.* ³⁰ *That day Moab was made subject to Israel, and the land had peace for eighty years.*

Small is the Next Big!

Let me show you the little things - the little instances of breakthrough where you're taking ground, getting healed, and learning to let go. You long for the big defining moment, the powerful encounter, and the light bulb to click on, but don't disregard the slow and steady changes, which happen over time and go deep within your heart and soul. Celebrate these small victories, recognize them and see them as incredibly significant. Because they are! It's in these seemingly small changes where the true and ultimate breakthrough takes place. Small is the next big!

_____

_____

_____

_____

_____

_____

_____

_____

_____

_____

1 Samuel 16:7

7 But the LORD said to Samuel, "Do not consider his appearance or his height, for I have rejected him. The LORD does not look at the things people look at. People look at the outward appearance, but the LORD looks at the heart."

July
Devotional

Let Me Be Your Checkpoint.

Let me be your checkpoint - your point of reference. The place where you first dial in and get your marching orders. Let me be your compass which points you due north and gives you a sense of true direction and perspective. Let me be the place where you reference back to – a check in spot where you come up for air and decide how to move forward. Let me be this place for you – a place of security, peace, and comfort – where you always know you're welcome and answers are sure to follow!

_____

_____

_____

_____

_____

_____

_____

_____

_____

_____

_____

_____

Psalm 32:8

[8] *I will instruct you and teach you in the way you should go;*
I will counsel you with my loving eye on you.

Don't Beat Yourself Up – Give Yourself Grace!

Why do you beat yourself up? Why are you so hard on yourself? I am not the one who's driving the hammer down on you, I am not the one who is holding the bar up higher and higher each day. That is not ME, so be sure that is also not YOU. Be kind to yourself, be quick to receive that compliment, and let yourself off the hook from time to time. You would never talk to a friend or child that way so why do you insist on beating yourself up. Decide today that you will love on YOU and be quick to give yourself grace.

_____
_____
_____
_____
_____
_____
_____
_____
_____
_____
_____

Acts 20:32

32 *"Now I commit you to God and to the word of his grace, which can build you up and give you an inheritance among all those who are sanctified.*

Let Me Breathe Afresh on Your Feelings Today.

I know you are upset and maybe downright angry, but first take a breath and come up for air. Allow me to show you the full perspective and give you fresh eyes on the situation. Allow me to lead the way and not your emotions which will only dig you a deeper hole. Put your feelings at my feet, and ask me to replace them with truth, love and grace. It's ok you feel that way, and in fact your emotions may even be valid, but that doesn't mean you need to react to them. Allow me to breathe afresh on your feelings today and you'll start to breath easier as well.

Psalm 119:30

30 I have chosen the way of faithfulness;
I have set my heart on your laws.

A Day of Freedom! Enjoy it!

A day of freedom to celebrate the sacrifice of so many. To honor their commitment and pay tribute to their faithfulness. It's no easy assignment, to leave your family not knowing if you'll return. To leave friendly environments and head into the most unfriendly of environments. To voluntarily walk away from what's cozy and comfortable and head into unfamiliar and unknown territory. Their sacrifice allows you to enjoy everyday life without concern that your life is in danger. So be thankful today for I've purposed the times and seasons and you are blessed to live in a land at such a time as this.

_____

_____

_____

_____

_____

_____

_____

_____

_____

_____

_____

_____

John 10:10

[10] *The thief comes only to steal and kill and destroy; I have come that they may have life and have it to the full.*

Faith, Hope, & Love Will Come Knocking at Your Door.

Faith will come knocking on your door. Hope will tap on your window. Love will sneak its way into your living room. All because I love you. All because I see you and I know what you need. Every inch of your house has my hand upon it. Every corner is surrounded by my goodness and grace. So when you hear the knocking, when you sense the tapping, and when kindness finds its way to each room, take time to STOP, let it in, embrace the moment, and allow faith, hope and love to enter your house again this day.

_____

_____

_____

_____

_____

_____

_____

_____

_____

_____

Psalm 25:5

⁵ Guide me in your truth and teach me,
for you are God my Savior,
and my hope is in you all day long.

There's NO Stopping You!

There's no stopping you. No stopping what you can't achieve, how high you can go, and the goals you want to reach. It may seem like a boulder is in your path. It may seem like the path ahead is completely fog-filled. It may seem like you're all alone on the journey. What it *seems like* is not your concern and is not where your focus should be. Set your heart on a destination, set your mind with determination, and set your hands to what I've placed in front of you. There's no stopping you, not me, not your friends or family, and especially not YOU!

Deuteronomy 31:23

²³ *The LORD gave this command to Joshua son of Nun:*
"Be strong and courageous, for you will bring the Israelites
into the land I promised them on oath, and I myself will be with you."

Where There's a Will, There's a Way.

Where there's a will, there's a way. You've heard it before. You've maybe even said it before. But what I want to know is do you believe it? Your will, your drive, your motivation, your focus, your tenacity, your determination, your endurance, and your perseverance. It's the inner resolve within you that says, "I will keep going. I won't stop. I won't give up. I won't back down from this challenge. I will, I will, I will." Where there's a will, there's a way and today as you step forward say, "I will," knowing that I AM *will* make a way.

_____

_____

_____

_____

_____

_____

_____

_____

_____

_____

_____

Psalm 119:58

58 I have sought your face with all my heart;
be gracious to me according to your promise.

Step Outside of the Box Today!

Don't be afraid of what's unfamiliar, what's a little awkward and what's beyond your comfort level. Different, unique and outside of the box just may be where I am deciding to live, breathe and move among you. It may be the very place where I want to show you my goodness, grace, and pour my abundance upon you. Don't be so quick to judge and so quick to toss what's "out there" aside. It may be the form in which I decide to show myself to you. Move forward carefully, noticing every detail and taking delight in the all the ways this pushes you out of your box and into this unfamiliar but soon to be familiar territory!

_____

_____

_____

_____

_____

_____

_____

_____

Deuteronomy 11:23-24
[23] *then the LORD will drive out all these nations before you,*
and you will dispossess nations larger and stronger than you.
[24] *Every place where you set your foot will be yours:*
Your territory will extend from the desert to Lebanon,
and from the Euphrates River to the Mediterranean Sea.

This Day will be Good Abundant & Full of Faith!

Every moment you have to decide which lens you'll view this day. Will it be good? Will it be faith-filled? Will it be joyful? The power is in simply deciding and being ruthless in your answer, and steadfast in your decision. Circumstances don't determine your internal world and they don't decide how your compass will read this day. You decide and become resilient in your mind – letting nothing get in your way of how you know you want to feel. Dig in deep, throw excuses out the window deciding that today - THIS DAY will be good, abundant and filled with faith!

_____

_____

_____

_____

_____

_____

_____

_____

_____

_____

_____

Psalm 100:5

⁵ For the LORD is good and his love endures forever;
his faithfulness continues through all generations.

Focus on Where I am Calling You!

Can it wait? Can it truly wait until tomorrow or next week or even the next? Imagine a week down the road, a month or even a year later and think how those decisions will shape your future. Take notice as to what and who are you investing in and where you are giving your time. Can it wait? I know it feels pressing, but is something else calling for your attention? Don't let the seemingly "good" distractions get in the way of where I am calling you!

_____
_____
_____
_____
_____
_____
_____
_____
_____
_____
_____
_____
_____
_____

Psalm 119:105

[105] *Your word is a lamp for my feet,*
a light on my path.

In the Seeking You Will Find!

Seek to understand, then to be understood. When you listen first, you're able to respond appropriately moving forward. Seek to learn and find out all the facts before you begin. There may be more that meets the eye, more under the surface. It may take a little digging, a little patience, and some time to settle into the full depth of the situation but remember there's no rush, only time to truly dig in and find the heartbeat of all that's going on. In the seeking you'll find, and in finding you'll understand, and this just may change everything.

Matthew 7:8

8 For everyone who asks receives; the one who seeks finds; and to the one who knocks, the door will be opened.

Remember You're Connected to the Ultimate Resource!

It's time to stand up. To fight for what you believe and who you believe in. To hold your ground, and not back down from the challenge in front of you. Your surroundings may look bleak, but remember you're connected to the Ultimate Resource. I have what you need and know when you need it. So stand up tall today, keep your head held high, and posture yourself in confidence. The road ahead will have bumps, turns, and detours, but I've called you to stand up tall because there are good things ahead!

_____

_____

_____

_____

_____

_____

_____

_____

_____

_____

_____

John 14:8
*8 Philip said, "Lord, show us the Father
and that will be enough for us."*

Grab the Freedom that is Yours!

Freedom is my desire for you. Inside and out, whole and healed - no barriers, no limits, and nothing holding you back. Only true freedom to run with your whole heart, soul and mind. I am lifting the restraints on you today, lifting what feels heavy and unbearable and giving you the freedom to advance. No more doubt, fear, and worry weighing you down, and no more self-sabotaging thoughts to keep you paralyzed from moving forward. Freedom is your word of the day – declare loudly, live it boldly, and never apologize for the freedom that is yours!

---

2 Corinthians 3:17

17 Now the Lord is the Spirit, and where the Spirit of the Lord is, there is freedom.

Let Me Be Your Navigational Guide!

Looking around everything looks disorganized, jumbled, and even the path ahead looks confusing. Nothing seems to have its place, and nothing fits where it's supposed, and, of course, nothing making sense BUT that's what I am for. The God who turns chaos into calm, showing you where things fit, how things go, and how I am right smack dab in the center of it all. Don't rush to clean it all up, trying to make things as perfect as you can. Let me be your navigational guide, and the one who gives you clarity and direction in the midst of the storm.

_____

_____

_____

_____

_____

_____

_____

_____

_____

_____

_____

_____

_____

Deuteronomy 8:2

2 Remember how the LORD your God led you all the way in the wilderness these forty years, to humble and test you in order to know what was in your heart, whether or not you would keep his commands.

What Do You Want? I Mean Really, Really Want?

What do you want? I mean, really, really want? At the core of your being I've placed desires, wants, and needs that are unique to you and you alone. I've crafted you for such a time as this. Take note of that crazy dream that keeps coming to your mind. Take note of the thoughts in your head that keep you up at night. I'll ask you again, "What do you want?" With all of your heart, mind, and soul what do you desire? It's in this place we are tapping into your destiny and stepping into divine greatness which is meant only for you and you alone!

_____

_____

_____

_____

_____

_____

_____

_____

_____

_____

_____

_____

Matthew 22:37

37 Jesus replied: "Love the Lord your God with all your heart and with all your soul and with all your mind."

This is about You – Don't Make it about Anyone Else.

This is about you - not your family, your parents, your kids, your friends, or your co-workers. It's about you. What steps you will take? What will you decide today? This is about you, your heart, mind, body and soul. Take every step with the end in mind, the future in front of you, and the past behind you. Cut out the excuses today and disregard the noise around you. It's you and me when you lay your head down and you and me when you arise each morning. This is about you – don't make it about anyone else.

_____

_____

_____

_____

_____

_____

_____

_____

_____

_____

_____

Luke 10:27

27 He answered, "'Love the Lord your God with all your heart and with all your soul and with all your strength and with all your mind'[a]; and, 'Love your neighbor as yourself.'[b] "

Just Breathe and Then Do the Next Thing.

Do not stop. Do not hold back. Do not give up when life gets hard, difficult, and confusing. Breathe deeply and then jump in. Do not give up when you hit the bottom but use it as a point to bounce back. Let it be the spring beneath your feet, and the foundation upon which you stand. Look ahead, move forward, even if it's at snail's pace. Keep going. Keep moving. Just don't stop!

Proverbs 21:1

21 *In the LORD's hand the king's heart is a stream of water that he channels toward all who please him.*

Stay Steadfast, Stay Resilient, and Stay Determined.

You can feel the change all around you - morning, noon, and night. There's a shift in the atmosphere, a movement and momentum taking place that you have nothing to do with. Your job is to stay in position, stay focused, and keep your eyes on the prize. Looking around nothing makes sense, but there's change beneath the surface and it's happening day by day. So stay steadfast, stay resilient, and stay determined with the goals in front of you. There's change in the atmosphere and soon you'll see it with your very eyes.

_____

_____

_____

_____

_____

_____

_____

_____

_____

Romans 8:24-25

*²⁴ For in this hope we were saved. But hope that
is seen is no hope at all. Who hopes for what they already
have? ²⁵ But if we hope for what we do not yet have,
we wait for it patiently.*

Stay Flexible Today and You'll Be Glad You Did.

Stay flexible. Stay moldable, teachable, and willing to bend with the circumstances around you. It doesn't mean you don't have an opinion or must bow to everyone else's needs. Instead easily respond to the situations in front of you so you are able to respond accordingly. Then you'll see what's needed, who needs your attention, and what adjustments need to be made. You'll see beyond the outside reality and into the hearts and minds of those around you, and quickly be able to "flex" your plans in order to adapt accordingly.

_____

_____

_____

_____

_____

_____

_____

_____

_____

_____

Jeremiah 33:6

6 *"'Nevertheless, I will bring health and healing to it;*
I will heal my people and will let them enjoy
abundant peace and security.

Let My Voice Drive Your Day.

Time is not your concern. You rush, you hurry – never feeling like you have enough time. Always wondering if you'll get in all done. But time should never be your concern. Time should never be what drives you and what determines your day. Let time be time, and let my Voice drive your day. Let love drive your focus, let grace drive your peace, and let grace remind you that there's always more than enough time. I am the watch keeper. I am the one that guides and directs your steps and knows just how much time you need. Don't let time rule you today. Let time be time, and I'll led your way!

Romans 8:38-39

[38] For I am convinced that neither death nor life, neither angels nor demons,[a] neither the present nor the future, nor any powers, [39] neither height nor depth, nor anything else in all creation, will be able to separate us from the love of God that is in Christ Jesus our Lord.

Open Your Eyes There's Always More That Meets the Eye.

Open your eyes today to new beginnings and new possibilities. There's a whole world in front of you to see from a fresh perspective. Ask me what I am doing and glean from new insight and revelation. Awake to all that's at your doorstep and let me show you my goodness. Allow yourself to be surprised by what you really see. Open your eyes today because there's always MORE that meets the eye.

_____

_____

_____

_____

_____

_____

_____

_____

_____

John 14:15-17

[15] *"If you love me, keep my commands.* [16] *And I will ask the Father, and he will give you another advocate to help you and be with you forever—* [17] *the Spirit of truth. The world cannot accept him, because it neither sees him nor knows him. But you know him, for he lives with you and will be[a] in you.*

You're Not a Failure –
You Must Keep Going.

If you think you've failed than you've missed the message entirely. You're not a failure, and your missteps haven't been failures. Failure is only when you give up. Every step, every movement is a chance to learn, to grow, and step into the fullness of all that's in front of you. If you're not learning than indeed you are moving backward, but I see you growing, thriving, and moving towards something incredible and in fact you are achieving it each and everyday. You are not a failure – keep going, keep learning and you'll see how great you already are!

John 15:16
16 You did not choose me, but I chose you and appointed you so that you might go and bear fruit fruit that will last and so that whatever you ask in my name the Father will give you.

Go on Then, Ask Me for Anything!

Ask me for the next thing - that next big or little thing on your list. The next need, the next provision, the next necessary thing to get you through the day, week, and month. Ask me and see how I provide. What's your next prayer request? What's the next opportunity you are hoping that shows up on your doorstep? What's the next thing you want on your wish list? There's no request that's too big or too small or seemingly too insignificant. If it's important to you, then it's important to me. Go on then, what are you waiting for? Ask me!

_____
_____
_____
_____
_____
_____
_____
_____
_____
_____
_____

John 16:14

14 He will glorify me because it is from me that
he will receive what he will make known to you.

Drop the Old Way and Step into the New!

This season is new, fresh, and full of opportunity. No longer can you operate in your old habits and old routines. These will leave you feeling lifeless and drained of all your energy. It's time to mix it up and do things differently. It's time to drop the familiar patterns and begin to tap into a new way of thinking, acting and behaving. Just because it's worked in the past doesn't mean it will work again. It's a fresh season and I have a new ways for you to operate which will give you the life, breath, and the energy you need. It's time to drop the old way and step into the NEW!

_____

_____

_____

_____

_____

_____

_____

_____

_____

_____

Job 8:7

7 Your beginnings will seem humble,
so prosperous will your future be.

Keep Feeding Your Hope – Again, Again and Again!

Today remember you carry hope. It's a feeling, desire, and emotion I've placed within you this day. Hope for the good, hope for the change, hope for the things you have yet to see happen, and hope for the completely unexpected. This is the hope within you today. Find it, tap into it, and search for it. When you find it, nurture it, grow it, and feed it. Again and again believe for what seems impossible. This feeling, this desire, this expectation although small now, can grow into something amazing – just keep feeding it – again and again and again!

_____

_____

_____

_____

_____

_____

_____

_____

_____

Psalm 63:3-4
³ Because your love is better than life,
my lips will glorify you.
⁴ I will praise you as long as I live,
and in your name I will lift up my hands.

223

Through the Grind It Will Always Be Worth It.

Life won't always be easy. Life won't always be smooth. Life won't always be filled with butterflies and fairy tales. Life isn't always sugar coated to your liking. How does an oyster form a pearl? Through trial, tension and a continual "rub" on life. This is where the magic happens and where something truly wonderful begins to take shape. Soon you'll look back and see you're being formed to my likeness and it's producing for you a tough outer shell to stand the storms ahead. Not only will you be protected, but also your beauty will draw many people to you. Life won't always be easy, but through the grind it will always be worth it!

_____

_____

_____

_____

_____

_____

_____

_____

Psalm 139:23-24

[23] Search me, God, and know my heart;
test me and know my anxious thoughts.
[24] See if there is any offensive way in me,
and lead me in the way everlasting.

Without a Doubt – You are on My Mind.

Without a doubt I am shaping you and molding you. Without a doubt I am crafting you day-by-day and hour-by-hour. Without a doubt you're the one who I love and seek to bless each day. Without a doubt you have a future of hope that awaits you. Without a doubt provision is set before you. You have all that you need, when you need it. My love covers you today and you'll be taken care of each and every day. Without a doubt, without question, and without hesitancy in my mind – my hand is over this day and every day after.

_____

_____

_____

_____

_____

_____

_____

_____

_____

Psalm 62:5-6

⁵ *Yes, my soul, find rest in God;*
my hope comes from him.
⁶ *Truly he is my rock and my salvation;*
he is my fortress, I will not be shaken.

Run After Your Freedom Today!

If freedom is what you desire, then freedom is what you must seek. Free from fear, free from doubt, and free from the opinions of others. Completely free from those voices in your head which yell, scream and shout accusations at you all day. Free to set yourself loose from the thoughts that bind you and the voices that entrap you. Cut them off, run the other way, and don't let them have any space in your life today. If freedom is what you desire, then take action and choose freedom today!

_____

_____

_____

_____

_____

_____

_____

_____

_____

_____

Galatians 5:13-14
[13] *You, my brothers and sisters, were called to be free.*
But do not use your freedom to indulge the flesh[a];
rather, serve one another humbly in love.
[14] *For the entire law is fulfilled in keeping*
this one command: "Love your neighbor as yourself."[b]

I am Expanding Your Capacity!

I am growing your capacity. I am growing the amount that you can handle, manage and eventually master. As you grow, you'll expand and stretch your limits, so you'll need to be quick to let go of the areas and responsibilities which are now not yours to carry. As your boundaries extend and your capacity grows, watch for the new responsibilities that I want to place in your lap. As life begins to look different let this be your confirmation that you're right where you're suppose to be. Let go of the old because I am expanding your capacity to make room for the new!

Jeremiah 29:11

[11] For I know the plans I have for you," declares the Lord,
"plans to prosper you and not to harm you,
plans to give you hope and a future.

Don't Forget to Laugh – Really Laugh!

Don't forget to laugh. Laugh about the little things, the big things and even the things that make you want to scream. Laugh, smile, chuckle, and don't forget that laughter really is the best medicine. It can calm your nerves, ease your pain, and remind you of the goodness that is all around you. Laughter can be your best friend in times where the world doesn't make any sense at all. So laugh today, a good ole deep belly laugh. Tell a joke, find a joke, watch a comedian, or share something funny. You'll smile, they'll smile and you'll both remember the benefit comes from pure innocent joy.

_____

_____

_____

_____

_____

_____

_____

_____

_____

_____

Job 8:21

*²¹ He will yet fill your mouth with laughter
and your lips with shouts of joy.*

It's Time for You to Believe in You!

It's time to act. Time to move. Time to go and time to put the pedal to the medal. No more waiting, no more hesitating and no more delays. Its time, *your time.* I believe in you, others believe in you and now it's time for *you to believe in you.* So get moving and start acting. Nothing is holding you back, nothing is keeping you from hitting that next level. You've planned enough, you've prepared enough and now you must put one foot in front of the other and advance! Acceleration is now what defines your days. The past is the behind you and the future is yours. Proceed my friend.

_____

_____

_____

_____

_____

_____

_____

_____

_____

_____

Hebrews 11:1-2

*¹ Now faith is confidence in what we hope for
and assurance about what we do not see.
² This is what the ancients were commended for.*

August
Devotional

Right Now Will Not Always Be, So Enjoy the Present.

Right now will not always be, for right now is right *now* – your present reality. Every day and every moment your world is being created in front of you. Don't get stuck thinking this season will last forever, BECAUSE IT WON'T. I know it seems like there's no end in sight, no solutions to be found and no relief around the corner, but remember today will not always be. Right now, is right now, and the future will look much different. No two seasons are the same, but each one is equally necessary. So enjoy right now because it won't always be.

_____

_____

_____

_____

_____

2 Peter 3:10-11

[10] *But the day of the Lord will come like a thief.*
The heavens will disappear with a roar; the elements
will be destroyed by fire, and the earth and
everything done in it will be laid bare.
[11] *Since everything will be destroyed in this way,*
what kind of people ought you to be?
You ought to live holy and godly lives

Keep Going Bit by Bit – Little by Little.

Keep going, bit by bit and little by little. Slowly but surely you will finish what you started. You haven't signed up to run the death sprint so why do you insist to live like you have. It's your internal reality, which creates for you a state of peace or a state of panic. Remind yourself that steady and constant is the victory of today and soon you'll hit the finish line with a smile on your face and energy for tomorrow!

Proverbs 28:20

20 *A faithful person will be richly blessed,*
but one eager to get rich will not go unpunished.

Ask for Wisdom to See More Clearly Today!

Take a closer look. Let your eyes look a little longer to see what's beneath the surface and look deeper allowing your senses to guide you further. A quick glance isn't always what it seems. Take a closer look at your circumstances, the situation you are in and the people around you. You might be surprised what you see and where your eye takes you. Your perspective might change, and your initial opinion might be altered. Take a closer look and ask for wisdom to see a little more clearly today.

_____

_____

_____

_____

_____

_____

_____

_____

_____

_____

_____

_____

Proverbs 2:6

⁶ For the LORD gives wisdom;
from his mouth come knowledge and understanding.

You're Worth Much More Than That.

There are some things not worth fretting over, some things not worth your attention, time, and energy. They steal your treasures, rob you of your joy, and kidnap your peace and leave you left out to dry. As these life occurrences find you again, let this time be different. As soon as they come, let them go. Don't entertain those thoughts that come through your mind which doesn't speak of truth and love. Fretting over something, which doesn't deserve your time or attention! You're worth much more than that!

Psalm 29:11
11 *The LORD gives strength to his people;*
the LORD blesses his people with peace.

Go Boldly and Confidently in the Direction of Your Dreams!

Are you ready to do something new? Something different? Something outside of the box? Something that scares you a little and pushes you out of your comfort zone? Are you ready for that? You might think you are anything but ready, yet the reality is I have prepared you for such a time as this. The years behind you, the months in the trenches, and the weeks of pure endurance have prepared you for this day. To step out for the first time in this new arena and go boldly and confidently in the direction of your dreams because you are more than ready. You've been destined for such a time as this!

_____

_____

_____

_____

_____

_____

_____

Esther 4:14

[14] *For if you remain silent at this time, relief and deliverance for the Jews will arise from another place, but you and your father's family will perish. And who knows but that you have come to your royal position for such a time as this?"*

Everyday Set Yourself Up for Success.

Everyday set yourself up for success. Everyday posture yourself so that opportunities and divine appointments come your way. Wake up with an ear to my voice as I show you the way. Position your meeting, your tasks, and everything in between with great purpose. Don't do anything just because you feel like it but instead seek to live with incredible intention. Organize your life around the larger goals I've placed in your heart and watch to see how I steadily show up in more ways than you can even ask or imagine. All because you decided to set yourself up for success!

_____

_____

_____

_____

_____

_____

_____

_____

_____

_____

_____

Exodus 14:13

[13] *Moses answered the people, "Do not be afraid. Stand firm and you will see the deliverance the LORD will bring you today. The Egyptians you see today you will never see again.*

It's Time to Step Out.

It's time to step out. Stepping out is an action, pointing you to where I want to go. It's not a passive thought you have in the day but rather a distinctive step that puts a line in the sand saying you will not hold back any longer. It's this simple act of faith and obedience letting go of something familiar that no longer fits you, so that you can step out into new territory!

_____

_____

_____

_____

_____

_____

_____

_____

_____

_____

_____

_____

_____

_____

Deuteronomy 19:8-9

[8] *If the LORD your God enlarges your territory, as he promised on oath to your ancestors, and gives you the whole land he promised them,* [9] *because you carefully follow all these laws, I command you today — to love the LORD your God and to walk always in obedience to him*

It's Time to Get Started.

It's time to get started. It's time to get the ball rolling and put one foot in front of the other. No more dragging your feet and no more excuses. It's time to get going. If you think something is holding you back, you are mistaken. There is no time like the present because you don't know what tomorrow will bring. You don't know what the future holds, and you don't want to look back with regret. So dive in today, 100% fully in. Even if you have to take your doubts, fears, and worries with you – GO FOR IT! It's time to get started and get the ball rolling!

Micah 3:8

8 *But as for me, I am filled with power,*
with the Spirit of the LORD,
and with justice and might,
to declare to Jacob his transgression,
to Israel his sin.

Let It Go Once Again.

Anyone can let go, once, twice, or even a couple times. The hard part comes in the daily deaths, the moment-by-moment breaths where you inhale and exhale letting go once again. It might be the 100th time that day, where you lay "it" down once again and more than likely that won't be the last time but here you go again releasing the burden, the hurt, the pain, the disappointment, and the confusion. It's not yours to hold onto, it's not yours to squeeze, and it's not yours to carry with you. In time, if you let it, it will be the cancer, which spreads, only keeping you captive to its grip. So, let go again and what's hard at first will get easier by the day, with every battle you fight, eventually you'll see the victory won.

Habakkuk 3:19

19 The Sovereign Lord is my strength;
he makes my feet like the feet of a deer,
he enables me to tread on the heights.

No More Thinking – Only Action.

D o it now. Yes, right now. Don't dwell on it. Don't think on it any longer. Nike said it best, "Just do it." Delaying, over thinking it and allowing it to play through your mind will drain you more than the actual act. Sooner than later make it happen so that you can move forward and get on with what's probably more important than that "thing" that's sitting over your head and weighing you down. No more thinking – only action. Go on then, get on it with it. Put this book down, pick up the phone, your car keys, your computer or whatever you need to make "it" happen and as Nike says, "Just do it."

_____

_____

_____

_____

_____

_____

_____

_____

_____

_____

2 Timothy 1:7

7 For the Spirit God gave us does not make us timid,
but gives us power, love and self-discipline.

Get Ruthless – Absolutely Ruthless Today.

Get ruthless today at following my voice. Ruthless at obeying it. Ruthless at finding joy throughout your day. Ruthless in loving the small things and truly appreciating the big things. Get ruthless. Be ruthless. Live ruthlessly. Let it be your way of life, which doesn't mean you plow over everybody and anybody that comes in your way. Instead get ruthless about the things that really matter and fight for your time and energy as if your life depends on it – because it does. Live ruthlessly today as you make space and time for those people, situations and the tasks which are of upmost importance.

_____

_____

_____

_____

_____

_____

_____

_____

_____

_____

Jeremiah 29:12

*12 Then you will call on me and come and pray
to me, and I will listen to you.*

Stay in Your Lane.

Stay in your lane. Work hard not to take those detours and get distracted by "traffic" that doesn't affect you. Stay in your lane and remain focused. You'll know when you are wandering outside your path because your load will become incredibly heavy, and fog will fill your path. Let me teach you today how to stick to your purpose, how to navigate the road I've designed you for and soon you'll be driving with ease and comfort. Stay in your lane today and let me pave the road before you!

_____

_____

_____

_____

_____

_____

_____

_____

_____

_____

Psalm 116:1-2

¹ I love the LORD, for he heard my voice;
he heard my cry for mercy.
² Because he turned his ear to me,
I will call on him as long as I live.

Pay Attention to Those Quick Passing Thoughts.

Momentarily you may have these passing thoughts. A quick voice in your head that seems to go out just as quickly out as it came in. Become great at noticing these momentary thoughts as they are attached to your destiny. These thoughts, which seem insignificant, are the very thoughts I want to awaken you to today. You might think of a co-worker to meet with, a friend to call, or a neighbor to pray for. You might think of a project to finally start, a task to re-engage with or a book to finally finish. Whatever the momentary thought know that my breath is behind it and attached to it is life, purpose and so much joy!

_____

_____

_____

_____

_____

_____

_____

_____

Philippians 4:8

⁸ *Finally, brothers and sisters, whatever is true,*
whatever is noble, whatever is right, whatever is pure,
whatever is lovely, whatever is admirable — if anything
is excellent or praiseworthy — think about such things.

What Feels Uncomfortable Will Soon Be Comfortable.

I am moving you beyond, beyond your limits, beyond your reservations and into new, exciting territory. At first it may be outside your understanding, outside your boundaries, and you'll feel stretched to the max. But let this be confirmation that I am moving you beyond your current condition and into new ground that will allow you to stretch your wings and fly. What at first feels uncomfortable will soon be comfortable and you'll even find yourself saying, "I am right where I am meant to be." So, enjoy today, be grateful right where you are because you won't be here long – I am moving you beyond these limits!

---

1 Corinthians 3:7
*7 So neither the one who plants nor the one who waters
is anything, but only God, who makes things grow.*

I See It All...So Let Go Today!

I know you're disappointed. I know you've been let down. I know you've had dreams shattered and hopes destroyed. I know, I've seen it and been with you through it all. Let me take your disappointment today. Let me take your hurt, anger and pain and properly dispose of it today. When not carefully managed these emotions are a dangerous weapon, ready to explode at any time. Give them to me today and allow me to replace them with my love, grace, and forgiveness. Once and for all say goodbye to those disappointments which still bind you and keep you locked up. I know all...so let it all go today!

Psalm 46:10

[10] *He says, "Be still, and know that I am God;*
I will be exalted among the nations,
I will be exalted in the earth."

It's Time You Start Building Again!

I t's time you start building again. Remember the foundation which brought you this far and begin to prepare the soil once again. Make ready your hands, your feet, and even your mind for what's ahead. With each step notice the lightness, the freshness, and the newness upon this hour. As you build this time it won't be like before with the heaviness and weight. Instead each step and task you complete will carry a power and authority that makes things fall into place. It's time to build, to truly put your heart, soul, and mind into your work and build the life you've been dreaming of. Don't be mistaken. It's time to start building!

_____

_____

_____

_____

_____

_____

_____

_____

_____

Isaiah 58:12
*12 Your people will rebuild the ancient ruins
and will raise up the age-old foundations;
you will be called Repairer of Broken Walls,
Restorer of Streets with Dwellings.*

It's a Win-Win When You Check In!

Check in today. Check in with me. Check in with the people you love. Check in with your friends, your family, and your co-workers. Check in with your neighbors. Find out how they are doing – how they are REALLY doing and take the time to listen and truly hear them today. A check in is more than a Hi – Bye – See You Later. It's an honest follow-up to see what's going on, what's good, what's hard, what's wonderful, and what's down right awful. So, check in today, check in with me, and with the ones you love. You'll be glad you did, and they will too! Remember it's a win-win when you check in!

_____

_____

_____

_____

_____

_____

_____

_____

_____

_____

1 John 4:21

²¹ *And he has given us this command:*
Anyone who loves God must also love their brother and sister.

Go Out of *Your* Way Today!

Go out of your way today. Yes, out of *your* way. It might be inconvenient. It might make your day even more chaotic and hectic but go the extra mile and you'll see it'll be worth it. You wouldn't have to, you could go on as a "business as usual" sort of day but be careful because you might just miss out on something amazing. Going out of your way means you mix it up and throw your personal agenda out the window. It means you're making others a priority and showing them the best way is to go out of *your* way!

_____

_____

_____

_____

_____

_____

_____

_____

_____

_____

Psalm 127:1

¹ Unless the LORD builds the house,
the builders labor in vain.
Unless the LORD watches over the city,
the guards stand watch in vain.

Don't Despise These Days of Toil.

Today you may need to plow, with your hands, your heart, and even your mind. To commit to the task at hand and the vision in front of you with a determination to dig into the obstacles that arise and forge ahead through the muck. It might be not always be easy, or fun, or even glamorous but understand that you are preparing the soil for what's to come. This day in and day out grind is required in order to make ready for what I have waiting for you. Do not despise these days of toil, for through them you will soon reap great rewards.

Revelation 2:2-3

[2] *I know your deeds, your hard work and your perseverance.*
I know that you cannot tolerate wicked people,
that you have tested those who claim to be apostles
but are not and have found them false. [3] *You have persevered*
and have endured hardships for my name and have not grown weary.

It's Time to Put the Spring Back in Your Step!

Are you ready to rebound and find yourself with life again? It's time to bounce back and not be bogged down any longer by past mistakes, past circumstances, or past scenarios. Are you ready to bounce back? This time you'll have momentum; this time you'll have speed, this time you'll accelerate with force, power and true authority. So, start bouncing, and allow yourself to spring to life once again. You'll find you will be ready, and the spring will surely be in your step.

_____

_____

_____

_____

_____

_____

_____

_____

_____

_____

Romans 5:5

⁵ And hope does not put us to shame, because God's love has been poured out into our hearts through the Holy Spirit, who has been given to us.

I am Your Support When You Need It Most.

I am your support when you need it the most. I am your help when the world screams at you. I am your compass when you aren't sure which way to go. I am here, I am behind you, I am ahead of you, and I am with you. Come and sit with me now. Let me hear what you have to say. You'll see I am your biggest fan, the one cheering you on and pushing you towards the finish line. You can do it and you are more than capable of all that's in front of you. Soon your goals will be met, your destination realized, and yours dreams a reality. Let me support you in this today.

Proverbs 18:10
¹⁰ The name of the LORD is a fortified tower;
the righteous run to it and are safe.

Let Me Lift That Weight Off Your Shoulders.

At some point what feels like a weight you can't lift off your shoulders, will all of a sudden be gone. You might not even know when it leaves or what caused it to vanish but soon you won't carry it any longer. The solution is to simply keep walking, keep in stride with me and you'll see how I work my magic. Your step will be lighter, and your heart will breathe easier. So, keep walking today, one foot in front of the other, however slow it may seem, because as we all know, the tortoise wins the race!

_____

_____

_____

_____

_____

_____

_____

_____

_____

Philippians 3:13-14

13 Brothers and sisters, I do not consider myself yet to have taken hold of it. But one thing I do: Forgetting what is behind and straining toward what is ahead,
14 I press on toward the goal to win the prize for which God has called me heavenward in Christ Jesus.

You're Doing It and I Couldn't Be Prouder of You!

Look back and reflect on how far you've come. Take a good hard look at all that has changed within you, around you, and be thankful. Celebrate the big and the small victories and everything in between. You wouldn't be where you are today without your consistent effort, your hard work, and your continual perseverance to keep going. Remember all that you've been through, all that has brought you to this moment, and be thankful for those that helped you get this far. You definitely wouldn't have made it without them, so call them, tell them thank you and give yourself a moment to breathe as you look back and reflect on not only my faithfulness but yours as well. You're doing it and I couldn't be prouder of you!

Romans 5:3-4

³ *Not only so, but we[a] also glory in our sufferings,*
because we know that suffering produces perseverance;
⁴ *perseverance, character; and character, hope.*

There's Hope in the Air, So Grab onto It!

With hope in the air, there's a feeling that anything is possible. Anything! Absolutely anything! Hope for your dreams to manifest, hope for that promotion to finally come through, hope for your health to have a breakthrough, and hope for your finances to get in order. There's hope and this hope starts in your voice. In speaking it out, in declaring that it WILL come to pass, and in pushing past your feelings and saying it anyway. Hope is something that starts at the tip of your tongue and in time your hope will become more than just something you say!

_____

_____

_____

_____

_____

_____

_____

_____

_____

_____

Hebrews 11:11

11 *And by faith even Sarah, who was past childbearing age, was enabled to bear children because she*[a] *considered him faithful who had made the promise.*

Each Day You are Creating the Life in Front of You.

What if you were persistent today? What if you were focused? What if you stayed diligent to the task at hand? What if you remained steadfast to the people around you? What if you decided to endure rather than give up? What would this look like? How would your day unfold? How would your actions look different? How would your conversation with others change? Lots of questions and only you have the answers. Decide how to live and how to pursue each day with incredible purpose. Understand that each and every day you're creating the life in front of you!

_____

_____

_____

_____

_____

_____

_____

_____

_____

_____

Psalm 90:12

[12] *Teach us to number our days,*
that we may gain a heart of wisdom.

Seek Out Wisdom from Those Who've Traveled Your Path.

Seek out wisdom from those who have already walked before you. Those who have lived life, who have a few grays hairs and have seen a thing or two. They may not have "the" answer, but they can shed light on your situation and can be a sounding board when you need it the most. You'll know these people by their fruit, by the peace they carry, and by the grace they can't help but to extend to you. If you find yourself a little uncomfortable with their answer let that be a sign. You're in the right place and they aren't going to sugar coat life for you. Seek out wisdom today, remembering it's often found in those who've traveled down your path.

Deuteronomy 32:7

7 Remember the days of old;
consider the generations long past.
Ask your father and he will tell you,
your elders, and they will explain to you.

Let Your Mind Race to those Good Thoughts Today.

Where is your mind going today? Where is your focus? What tape is on repeat in your head? Is it thoughts of love or thoughts of hate? Remember, what you think on is where you'll eventually end up. It's as complicated and as simple as that. So, start your day thinking on that which builds you up and when the storms of life happen be quick to bring uplifting thoughts back again. Because what you think on will soon become your reality!

_____

_____

_____

_____

_____

_____

_____

_____

_____

_____

_____

_____

Deuteronomy 30:19

[19] *This day I call the heavens and the earth as witnesses against you that I have set before you, life and death, blessings and curses. Now choose life, so that you and your children may live.*

It's Time to Get After It.

Do you want something? No, do you truly want something? Maybe a desire, a goal, a New Year's Resolution you've had forever? What is it? What do you want? What do you crave? Put down your excuses and set aside the buts, if onlys, and maybe somedays. It's time to get after it. To determine in your heart, soul, body and that you will go after it. I can hear you doubting, wondering, and worrying if you have what it takes and if this time could really be different. But hear me now when I say, "It can, it will, and it is!" Start moving forward and get after it, no more waiting for that perfect time - *that* time doesn't exist. It's only **now**, right in front of you. It's yours to cease!

_____

_____

_____

_____

_____

_____

_____

_____

_____

_____

Romans 13:11

[11] *And do this, understanding the present time: The hour has already come for you to wake up from your slumber, because our salvation is nearer now than when we first believed.*

You are an Original, So Let Yourself Shine!

You aren't like everyone else. You never have been, and you never will be. You are an original who's uniquely made for such a time as this. I knew you would be perfect for this specific time period and perfect for the place you are currently living and perfect for the people all around you. The specific gifts and talents I have placed within you set you up for such a time as this! Of course, that doesn't mean that everything will always be perfect, but make no mistake I haven't made one mistake in you. As you take pursuit of what I've put in your heart, you'll see just how perfect you really are!

_____

_____

_____

_____

_____

_____

_____

_____

_____

_____

Ecclesiastes 3:1
¹ There is a time for everything,
and a season for every activity under the heavens:

I Give You Permission to Indulge in Those Good Things.

Today I give you permission to indulge in those good things which you love…maybe a decadent chocolate, a hot bubble bath, a good book and a fine wine, or splurging on your favorite restaurant. Whatever "it" is I give you permission to ENJOY yourself and the wholesome pleasures I have put within you. Don't waste your time feeling guilty, but instead allow yourself the opportunity to take delight in those things which bring you happiness and satisfaction. It brings me much delight when I see a smile upon your face as you delight in the desires of your heart.

Psalm 118:24

²⁴ The LORD has done it this very day;
let us rejoice today and be glad.

Let Your Day Be Filled with Hope, Joy and Expectation!

Y ou can get excited. Yes, excited! Maybe it's a promotion, a favorite show that's finally back on the air, or maybe an extra vacation day. It can be something big, something little or something in between – either way let yourself be filled with JOY, HOPE, and EXPECTATION that good things are on their way. Maybe you're waiting for the ball to drop or expecting the worst, but you're waiting in vain and missing the opportunity to let your heart fully feel and for joy to bubble up once again. So, get excited today about the big and the little things for it's all worth celebrating. Don't let this opportunity pass you by!

_____

_____

_____

_____

_____

_____

_____

_____

_____

_____

Psalm 94:19

[19] *When anxiety was great within me,*
your consolation brought me joy.

September
Devotional

There's a Shift on the Horizon.

There's a shift on the horizon. There's movement in the air. You may not be able to see it, but know I am at work on your behalf because it's time. Time to move. Be open to my voice and trust in my timing. The doors will open at the right time and in the right place and my provision will be waiting for you. Even when you can't see it or feel, it there's movement, growth and expansion taking place. What's to come will exceed your wildest expectations. You only need to trust in my goodness and day-by-day you'll see my plans unfolding.

_____

_____

_____

_____

_____

_____

_____

_____

_____

_____

_____

_____

2 Samuel 7:28

²⁸ Sovereign LORD, you are God! Your covenant is trustworthy,
and you have promised these good things to your servant.

Trust the Growth You Can't Always See.

When a seed is planted you can't see it growing but you trust the roots are being established and soon it will prosper and flourish. In the same way trust in my wisdom that I am growing you beneath the surface and at just the right time a harvest will sprout for you. My desire is that you're roots would sink deep, so that when the storms come you will be able to stand firm and even others will draw upon your strength. I am a God who is on the move, who's working on your behalf, growing you deep within so that you're ready for my gift of blessings. Trust there is growth you can't always see!

Luke 17:5-6

⁵ The apostles said to the Lord, "Increase our faith!" ⁶ He replied, "If you have faith as small as a mustard seed, you can say to this mulberry tree, 'Be uprooted and planted in the sea,' and it will obey you.

I am More Powerful than You Know.

Y ou can't see the wind, yet you feel its breeze. To "see it" is to watch how it effects the environment around you and the people around you. This is how I move. Pay attention to where the breeze blows, where goodness follows, grace enters, and love ushers in. Here you'll see where I am moving, and how I desire to act. I shift environments. I transform the hearts of many. I am more powerful than any wind and I hope you never forget...*this* is the power that resides in you.

_____

_____

_____

_____

_____

_____

_____

_____

_____

_____

1 Thessalonians 1:4-5

⁴ For we know, brothers and sisters[a] loved by God,
that he has chosen you,⁵ because our gospel came to you
not simply with words but also with power, with the
Holy Spirit and deep conviction. You know how
we lived among you for your sake.

Giving Up is Not in Your DNA.

Giving up is not in your DNA. I designed you with a fight, a resolve, and a tenacity that does not quit. You are meant for the battles and you will come out victorious with your head held high. This is who you are and how I've created you. I have gone before you and there is nothing you can't handle. My nature within you gives you the strength, endurance, and stamina to put one foot in front of the other and keep going. This is how you battle, moment by moment, as I release all you need each and every day. You are a fighter, a warrior, and the one who won't back down. This is who you are!

_____

_____

_____

_____

_____

_____

_____

_____

_____

_____

2 Corinthians 4:16

16 Therefore we do not lose heart. Though outwardly we are wasting away, yet inwardly we are being renewed day by day.

Keep Trusting for There's Movement Beneath the Surface.

When life feels desolate and barren and void of promise, it's here where your foundation and your roots grow deeper. Here there's movement beneath the surface and I am working where you can't see. Here the most crucial elements are actually being created so that you will be able to go further and farther than you could ever imagine. Trust the process, trust every step of the way and when it looks like nothing is going on, remember my faithfulness to you. Just when you're ready to call it quits, my goodness is shown, and your hope is restored. Keep trusting, for there's movement beneath the surface.

_____

_____

_____

_____

_____

_____

_____

_____

_____

Revelation 21:5

⁵ He who was seated on the throne said, "I am making everything new!" Then he said, "Write this down, for these words are trustworthy and true."

Let My Goodness Wash Over You Today.

Let my goodness wash over you today. Let it seep through your bones and awake your soul. It's here where the thirsty, barren, and weak come again and again. I will refresh you today. I will give you what you need. I will overwhelm you with my grace and compassion. I will fill you with joy as you stand in my presence. I will fulfill my promises to you. I will because I AM. I AM the God who supplies everything you need. Position yourself for my grace, for it's yours for the taking.

_____
_____
_____
_____
_____
_____
_____
_____
_____
_____

Romans 3:22-24
²² This righteousness is given through faith in[a] Jesus Christ to all who believe. There is no difference between Jew and Gentile, ²³ for all have sinned and fall short of the glory of God, ²⁴ and all are justified freely by his grace through the redemption that came by Christ Jesus.

I See You and Have Good Setup for You Today.

I see you my child. This day is not like any other day. It's unique in form and nature and there are opportunities waiting for you to step into. Look ahead with an expectation of what I might do, where I might lead you and how I might be at work. Yesterday is gone but the present is before you. Don't assume you have it all figured out, but be steady on my voice anticipating miracles throughout the day. I am a Father who has your absolute best in mind. I am at work on your behalf even when you can't see it. I see you my child and have glory for you today.

_____

_____

_____

_____

_____

_____

_____

_____

_____

_____

James 4:6

⁶ *But he gives us more grace. That is why Scripture says:*
"God opposes the proud
but shows favor to the humble.

Let Me Re-Direct You Back to My Voice.

All around you there is competition for your time and attention. The radio, TV, social media, as well as your co-workers, family and friends are all asking for you to tune into them. Some of these voices may even be good and encouraging but so quickly the noise becomes exhausting and overwhelming. Today, as your loving Father I am re-directing your attention back to my Voice, which is always full of peace, joy, hope and love. This is the Voice which will be your guide and will never steer you wrong.

Hebrews 4:16

[16] *Let us then approach God's throne of grace with confidence, so that we may receive mercy and find grace to help us in our time of need.*

There is Beauty and Life All Around You.

There is beauty all around you and there is life coming to the surface that is ready to burst. This is your true reality - a life full of opportunity, brimming with faith, with grace at every doorstep. As you walk forward there are flowers to pick, aromas to smell and love to grab onto. There's a destiny that covers your life and a protection that I command over your coming and your going. When I say, "I see you," it means no good thing is ever withheld from you. My nature is to give, to pour out my abundant blessing in hopes that you might prosper. This is the reality I long for you to live in each and every day.

Psalm 145:16

*16 You open your hand
and satisfy the desires of every living thing.*

When You're Ready to Speak, I am Listening.

Listening is an art and not everyone you meet is a good listener, but don't forget I am the best listener there is. When life feels chaotic and full of noise know that I am ready to hear you. I not only hear the words, but I feel their weight, their heaviness, and their depth. I understand the emotion, feeling, joy and pain behind each sentence. Come to me today and pour out your heart and let me truly listen to everything you're saying. I won't be offended, I won't be surprised, and I won't be angry. So, speak to me today for I am ready to listen.

_____

_____

_____

_____

_____

_____

_____

_____

_____

_____

_____

1 Peter 3:12

¹² For the eyes of the Lord are on the righteous
and his ears are attentive to their prayer,
but the face of the Lord is against those who do evil."

It's Time to Jump!

I have equipped you to jump. To spring forward into your destiny and step into the places I have called you. Taking a leap of faith may seem scary, terrifying and even at times keep you paralyzed but risk taking is where we thrive together. I've designed you to be creative and to continuously step out in faith. You are ready. You have what you need, and I will provide what's necessary for the journey ahead. The doors are opening, and the opportunities are in front of you. This is just the beginning. The new chapter is being written as we speak. It's time to JUMP!

_____

_____

_____

_____

_____

_____

_____

_____

Galatians 2:20-21

*20 I have been crucified with Christ and I no longer live,
but Christ lives in me. The life I now live in the body,
I live by faith in the Son of God, who loved me and gave
himself for me. 21 I do not set aside the grace of God,
for if righteousness could be gained through the law,
Christ died for nothing!"*

I am Your Father, the Builder of Your Life.

I am a builder. The very nature of who I am is to create, expand, and advance. I can help and want to add blessing and substance to your life. I am the great architect who formed this earth from nothing and made you from the dust of the ground. I build every detail of your life and when you look around seeing chaos or darkness that's your queue I am about to move. I am surveying the land around you, taking spiritual inventory of what's available, and getting ready to launch my resources in order to build on your life. This is who I am, and this is what I do. I am your Father, the builder of your life.

_____

_____

_____

_____

_____

_____

_____

_____

Psalm 37:5-6
⁵ Commit your way to the LORD;
trust in him and he will do this:
⁶ He will make your righteous reward shine like the dawn,
your vindication like the noonday sun.

Don't Stop Until You Find the Gold.

Awaken today to who I truly am. Not who the world says I am or what your friends, family or co-workers say about me, but truly to the heartbeat of my nature. Get to know me as Love, Peace, and Joy. Look for me in people and as you go about your day and pay attention to where I am moving and how I want to shower you with my goodness. Don't settle for displays of me that aren't in fact me, but rather seek me as if you're looking for hidden treasure and don't stop until you find the gold!

Proverbs 4:6-7

⁶ Do not forsake wisdom, and she will protect you;
love her, and she will watch over you.
⁷ The beginning of wisdom is this: Get wisdom.
Though it cost all you have, get understanding.

Your Nature is Peace, Love, Joy & Kindness.

Your nature is peace, love, joy, kindness, and self-control. This is who you are and how I've created you. Every thread and fiber of your being is marked by an element of my goodness and grace. There's no defect in you, no mistake about you, and nothing is out of place. You are designed by a perfect Creator and walk in my perfection. As you go about your day, cast aside anxiety, fear, doubt, and worry and look for opportunities to step into faith, hope and love. With every second that goes by I am waiting, ready to release exactly what you need at the proper time. Trust in who I am but also trust in *who I am in you!*

_____

_____

_____

_____

_____

_____

_____

_____

Colossians 3:9-10

[9] *Do not lie to each other, since you have taken off your old self with its practices* [10] *and have put on the new self, which is being renewed in knowledge in the image of its Creator.*

Hang Tight Because I am About to Breakthrough.

It's at the point of greatest tension where I am able to breakthrough. With your eyes locked on the target, with your fingers gripped firmly around the bow, you can feel the tension. This is the moment when you aren't sure if you can remain in this place of resistance any longer. But hang on and endure a little longer and soon there will be a quick release and a moment of acceleration. Let go of distractions, and allow God to keep expanding your vision, all the while keeping your eyes locked on the target because you're about to be released!

_____

_____

_____

_____

_____

_____

_____

_____

_____

_____

_____

_____

Job 17:9

⁹ *Nevertheless, the righteous will hold to their ways,*
and those with clean hands will grow stronger.

I am Creating for You a New Normal.

I am creating for you a new normal. A normal that goes beyond your limits or what you perceive as your limits. This normal sets the bar higher and raises the standards for how you see and live. It's a normal that is sustainable, maintainable, and full of incredible life. This is a normal you've been longing for and are in fact ready for. It's time to let go of old habits, old ways, and old thinking and take on my , my thinking, and my behavior. With one step in front of the other, I'll create your new normal. Day-by-day giving you the life, you've been destined for!

_____

_____

_____

_____

_____

_____

_____

_____

_____

_____

_____

John 8:12

¹² *When Jesus spoke again to the people, he said, "I am the light of the world. Whoever follows me will never walk in darkness but will have the light of life."*

I Don't Miss a Thing!

I don't miss a thing. Nothing is hidden from my sight. I look at you and see your whole life, your whole existence and it excites me. You haven't missed anything, and you haven't lost your footing. It's quite the opposite. You are on solid ground if you walk with me as I see your every move and help you along the way. When you look back with doubts and insecurities of what was or what might have been, I am already looking ahead ready to bless you abundantly and show you my faithfulness. I am guiding your path so that you don't miss anything – NOT ONE THING!

1 Timothy 6:12

*12 Fight the good fight of the faith. Take hold of the
eternal life to which you were called when you made
your good confession in the presence of many witnesses.*

Trust Me Today I am Crafter It All Before You.

I am your crafter. All around you I am building new plans, new connections, new alignments, and new opportunities. I am the ultimate creator of your life and not only do I give you solid foundations to stand on, but I add beautiful intricate details to grow and expand your horizons. There are no limits over you, no ceiling above your head and no barriers around you. There's only me, paving the way before you as I help create your life. I see from the beginning to the end and know how to connect the dots in between so you stay perfectly aligned. Trust me today. I am crafting it all before you.

Psalm 33:18

[18] *But the eyes of the LORD are on those who fear him,*
on those whose hope is in his unfailing love.

Wake Up with Me – I am Ready to Meet with You.

Wake up today and look around you. I am in the little moments of the day. I am waiting for you, anticipating your every move and positioning myself to meet you each step of the way. I don't look down at you. No, I walk with you in the here and the now – right along side of you. As you move, I move - in sync we move together. Living as one, it's here where my presence is revealed, and you come alive like never before. So wake up today with me in mind, knowing I am scheduled to meet you every moment of the day.

Proverbs 24:14
14 Know also that wisdom is like honey for you:
If you find it, there is a future hope for you,
and your hope will not be cut off.

Nothing is Hidden from My Sight.

It's time. The seasons are changing and there is movement around you. Everywhere you look, you'll start to see my light guiding the way. I am for you and with you and pave the road ahead of you. There is no need to worry, no need to fret as I see the details, and I live in both big and small details of life. Look upon this day with expectation of how I might move and where I might act. My faithfulness never leaves you and you can bank on my promises. There's movement in the air, even when you can't see it – make no mistake of that because nothing is hidden from my sight.

Isaiah 58:11
¹¹ *The LORD will guide you always;*
he will satisfy your needs in a sun-scorched land
and will strengthen your frame.
You will be like a well-watered garden,
like a spring whose waters never fail.

Change is on the Way.

With a change in the season you can expect change on the way. Be attentive to my voice, my leading, and my promptings. I come in unexpected packages, but you will know it's me when the spirit within you jumps, leaving you with a deep resounding peace that surpasses all circumstances. Moving forward your steps will be light. They won't always be easy but as I walk with, you'll always find the journey more than worth it. Remember my gifts are different from the world as I give you things the world cannot. You'll be left with peace, joy, hope and love, and remembering the greatest of these is love.

_____

_____

_____

_____

Psalm 1:1-3

¹ Blessed is the one
who does not walk in step with the wicked
or stand in the way that sinners take
or sit in the company of mockers,
² but whose delight is in the law of the LORD,
and who meditates on his law day and night.
³ That person is like a tree planted by streams of water,
which yields its fruit in season
and whose leaf does not wither –
whatever they do prospers.

Push the Boundaries, Expand Your Limits – Your Time is Now!

Push the boundaries and expand your limits because I am doing a new thing. A new season is upon you which will stretch you and draw you out further and farther. Say, "no" to the limits around you and "no" to the ceilings over your head. You are meant to fly and meant for the outer gates. When I say there is no limit on you, it means you can run unhindered and dance without reservations. Your time of hiddenness is over. It's time to break forth knowing you're meant to push the boundaries and meant to soar the skies.

_____

_____

_____

_____

_____

_____

_____

_____

_____

_____

Proverbs 6:23
²³ For this command is a lamp,
this teaching is a light,
and correction and instruction
are the way to life.

Let Love Be Your Anchor.

When love is your anchor there's nothing that can penetrate this bond, and this unity. Love remains the cornerstone, the foundation, and the expression of all I am and do. This love is powerful, radiant, and stronger than anything you can see in this world. I am inviting you to deeper levels of love which will be the fuel to wake you up each morning, the power you'll need throughout the day, and the peace to give your soul rest at night. So, let love be your anchor and you'll always be grounded yet ready to fly.

_____

_____

_____

_____

_____

_____

_____

_____

_____

_____

Hebrews 6:19-20

19 *We have this hope as an anchor for the soul,*
firm and secure. It enters the inner sanctuary behind the curtain,
20 *where our forerunner, Jesus, has entered on our behalf.*
He has become a high priest forever, in the order of Melchizedek.

Remember My Burden is Light.

Are the expectations of others overwhelming you? Does the responsibility within and around you seem too great? Does the weight of the world feel like it's on your shoulders? My dear, this is not from me for my burden is light. As a father who loves his child I long to remove the chains which cause you to grow weary. I haven't asked you to carry more than you can handle. You have permission to say no to the tasks and people I haven't asked you to walk with. I give you power, grace, and wisdom when you need it, and it's my delight to see you move forward with the breeze of a feather. Remember *my burden* is light.

_____

_____

_____

_____

_____

_____

_____

_____

_____

_____

_____

Matthew 6:27

²⁷ Can any one of you by worrying add a single hour to your life?

Come Now, for I Invite You to Rest.

It's in the calm of the storm where I invite you to rest. To find my heartbeat, find the stillness of the hour and invite peace to enter in. It's not some new age formula of meditation but rather an invitation to allow me to sit next to you. My concern is for your heart, the inner pulse where life first begins. Here in the midst of the chaos I remind you of your true north – the place where the chaos stops and stillness rushes in. Sit with me now as the storm whirls around you and watch how I calm the waters.

Psalm 107:28-30

[28] *Then they cried out to the LORD in their trouble,*
and he brought them out of their distress.
[29] *He stilled the storm to a whisper;*
the waves of the sea were hushed.
[30] *They were glad when it grew calm,*
and he guided them to their desired haven.

Know that I am Coming to Fill.

W hen there's space in your life know that I am coming to fill it. Don't try to fill it with your own agenda and tasks but wait on my move. You'll know when you're out of step with my leading and when you're moving forward in your own strength. I make a way where there is no path, and I create opportunities when situations look hopeless. I formed this earth from nothing because my name and nature is Creator. As you look at the space around you, don't see it as barren instead look with expectation of how I am about to *create* new blessings in your life.

_____

_____

_____

_____

_____

_____

_____

_____

_____

_____

_____

Psalm 20:4

*⁴ May he give you the desire of your heart
and make all your plans succeed.*

There's a Consistency Coming.

There's a consistency coming and a sharpening of your focus on *whom* I am drawing towards you and *what* I am drawing you towards. As I narrow your vision you can move forward with a confidence that your steps are sure footed, and your path will be laid before you. Your eyes will be aimed for your desired destination and it's in this place, that I am drawing you closer to hear my voice. Soon you'll step into this new place of consistency, soon you'll see this vision begin to manifest, and soon the mud you've walked through will all make sense.

_____

_____

_____

_____

_____

_____

Jeremiah 17:7-8

7 *"But blessed is the one who trusts in the LORD,*
whose confidence is in him.
8 *They will be like a tree planted by the water*
that sends out its roots by the stream.
It does not fear when heat comes;
its leaves are always green.
It has no worries in a year of drought
and never fails to bear fruit."

I Work Everything for Your Good.

Trust is more than a feeling, an emotion or surge of the soul. It forms within your heart and bubbles up within, and eventually finds an outlet in the souls of your feet. As you begin to walk in this trust your confidence grows knowing you have a Father in Heaven who resides in the future and works everything for your good. This is the trust you carry, as your feelings become more than emotions, as they live and breath and bless the world around you.

_____

_____

_____

_____

_____

_____

_____

_____

_____

_____

_____

_____

_____

_____

_____

Exodus 14:14

¹⁴ *The LORD will fight for you; you need only to be still.*

I Have Your Best in Mind – Your Absolute Best.

I am the Master of the clock. I am the Master of time. I know when it's time to go, time to stay, and time to change directions. With every second that goes by I am aware of what must happen; as nothing is missed from my eye. As the Master I have your best in mind, your absolute best. You may be waiting, anticipating and crying out for change, but rest in my knowledge that I see everything. Every detail is accounted for, every step is counted, and every move is perfectly calculated. Trust in my greater perspective and my greater awareness that my timing is perfect.

_____

_____

_____

_____

_____

_____

_____

_____

_____

_____

_____

1 John 5:14

[14] *This is the confidence we have in approaching God:*
that if we ask anything according to his will, he hears us.

Family is What I am Building.

Family is what I am building. Family is who I am. I have made you for relationship; I have made you for community, to do life with one another. Family is who you battle for, who you fight for and the ones you dig in your heels for because someone in your family needs what you have. If you're thinking, "Who needs me?" then you're right where you're suppose to be and God's about to move. Most days this intimacy might be awkward, weird, and uncomfortable but in the end, I am moving you to a place where you're growing in family together and nothing can separate this love that binds you all.

_____

_____

_____

_____

_____

_____

_____

_____

_____

_____

_____

Exodus 20:12

¹² *"Honor your father and your mother, so that you may live long in the land the LORD YOUR GOD IS GIVING YOU.*

October
Devotional

There's Significance in the Voice You Carry.

There's significance in the voice you carry. The sound, the tone, the vibrations of each word have meaning, life, and wisdom. What you say has the power to break or power to mend. How you decide to use this gift is up to you. I am ready to speak through you, ready to be the voice within your voice. We are one, unified, and in sync. Don't forget it's my nature living in you that has authority beyond anything or anyone in this world, so that nothing is impossible.

Matthew 19:26

26 Jesus looked at them and said, "With man this is impossible, but with God all things are possible."

Run, Run, Run to My Presence.

Run, run, run to my presence. When life comes at you and you feel overwhelmed and unsure of where or how to turn, run to me. I am here, now and always, and want to meet you and embrace you. If doubts, worries, and anxieties overtake you, again it's me you can run to you. I am a shelter, a strong tower, a refuge in time of need. Awaken to my presence and look at me again. Turn your eyes to me. The world would have you engage with the chaos, but I am the calm in the storm. I am the one who can give your heart peace when the wind blows, and the rain hits hard. Run to me child and find rest for your soul.

_____

_____

_____

_____

_____

_____

Psalm 31:1-2
[1] *In you, LORD, I have taken refuge;*
let me never be put to shame;
deliver me in your righteousness.
[2] *Turn your ear to me,*
come quickly to my rescue;
be my rock of refuge,
a strong fortress to save me.

If Love is Your Heartbeat, then You'll Never Miss a Beat.

If love is your heartbeat, then you'll never miss a beat. You won't worry about the path ahead and the obstacles that may come. Instead you'll rest in my goodness, my grace, and my understanding. Love is patient, always kind and full of compassion. It never boasts but is always most concerned about the well-being of others. Its focus is on blessing, giving, and igniting purpose. This love you must fight for, strive for, and also rest in. It's available all day, every day and takes care of you throughout the day. This love is found in a person - His name is Jesus and His heartbeat is love.

---

1 John 3:1

[1] *See what great love the Father has lavished on us,*
that we should be called children of God! And that is what we are!
The reason the world does not know us is that it did not know him.

Don't Dwell on Yesterday – Today is a New Day!

It's a new day. Don't dwell on yesterday, don't look back and think of what could have been, might have been, or should have been. I see the fullness of today, the possibilities of every opportunity - they are endless and knocking at your door. This is the beauty of a new day. It's a fresh start and a new beginning with powerful choices that I've designed for you because I trust you. As you step out in faith, my goodness will meet you there. No longer will you look back with despair but now today with eyes forward a hope is building in you - a hope that pushes out the fear, worry, and sorrow and fills your soul. Remember this day, your NEW day.

_____

_____

_____

_____

_____

_____

_____

_____

_____

Romans 15:13
[13] *May the God of hope fill you with all joy and peace as you*
trust in him, so that you may overflow with hope
by the power of the Holy Spirit.

I am With You. I am With You. I am With You.

I am with you. I am with you. I am with you. These are not just empty words I say in passing. These are words that carry power and meaning. When I say I am with you it means my presence goes before you, my Love builds within you, and my watchful eye protects you. When you're standing next to someone you love, you can feel their presence. This is how close I am, how near I am when you need me. Come to me, knowing that I am ready to give you what you need every minute of the day. It's in these moments you'll experience the reality that I am with you, I am with you, I am with you.

_____

_____

_____

_____

_____

Hebrews 13:5-6

[5] *Keep your lives free from the love of money and be content with what you have, because God has said,*
"Never will I leave you;
never will I forsake you." [a]
[6] *So we say with confidence,*
"The Lord is my helper; I will not be afraid.
What can mere mortals do to me?" [b]

I Give Strength to the Weary
and Hope to the Restless.

When you're tired and worn out and when you want to check out from the world, this is when you must come running to me. I give strength to weary and hope to the restless. Don't push forward in your own efforts only to burn out. Sit at my feet, listen to my voice, and trust in my leading. In that moment, I'll come; I'll fill and expand your capacity for every ounce of energy you need. Don't be dismayed any longer for I am ready to release all you need.

_____

_____

_____

_____

_____

_____

_____

_____

_____

_____

Romans 8:28-29

[28] *And we know that in all things God works for the good of those who love him, who have been called according to his purpose.* [29] *For those God foreknew he also predestined to be conformed to the image of his Son, that he might be the firstborn among many brothers and sisters.*

It's in the Preparation Where I am Wildly at Work.

Prepare your heart, open your mind, and ready your soul. It's in the preparation where I am wildly at work as the pieces fall into place in order to connect to your greater purpose. This time of development and planning is crucial for what's ahead. Although the tasks might be tedious and the steps even mundane, make no mistake that I am at work and a foundation is being set. Here in the present is where I am readying your heart, soul, and mind giving you the wisdom that qualifies you for your destiny ahead.

_____

_____

_____

_____

_____

_____

_____

_____

Psalm 3:3-5
³ But you, LORD, are a shield around me,
my glory, the One who lifts my head high.
⁴ I call out to the LORD,
and he answers me from his holy mountain.
⁵ I lie down and sleep;
I wake again, because the LORD sustains me.

305

It's Darkest Before the Dawn.

Before the dawn is when it's darkest, with not an ounce of light piercing through. In this place you must wait and rest on my promises, knowing that I am faithful and good. Going forward may look scary and even as you look back you may not be able to see how you got here, but trust that opportunity stands in front of you. Trust in my perfect timing, knowing the light will soon come and understanding is about to break through, as its darkest just before the dawn.

Matthew 4:16

[16] *the people living in darkness
have seen a great light;
on those living in the land of the shadow of death
a light has dawned.*[a]

The God You Know is Good!

Don't stop believing in the goodness around you. The world, the media, even co-workers and family members with good intent can be a voice of discouragement when all you need is truth, hope and love. There's no stopping the abundance and blessing I want to pour out to you. It doesn't always look like fancy cars and white picket fences and all that glitters, but it's my goodness that covers you, protects you, and allows your senses to come alive like never before. When the world is screaming at you to lose hope, this is your opportunity to do the opposite and shout from the bottom of your lungs, "The God I know is GOOD!"

_____

_____

_____

_____

_____

_____

_____

_____

_____

_____

Nahum 1:7

⁷ *The LORD is good,*
a refuge in times of trouble.
He cares for those who trust in him,

My Heart is to Connect with You.

My heart is to connect with you. It's intimacy that I am longing for - to hear your heart and understand your every thought and emotion. What I most enjoy is my time with you. Your voice, your personality and everything that makes you, YOU! Your heart is my concern because it's here where life flows, and where my presence flows out. So, sit at my feet and know it's your heart that I seek.

_____

_____

_____

_____

_____

_____

_____

_____

_____

_____

_____

_____

_____

_____

_____

_____

_____

Matthew 6:21

21 For where your treasure is, there your heart will be also.

I Wake Up With You in Mind.

I wake up with you in mind each and every day. You're always in my thoughts. There's nothing I see in your day that I haven't planned for you. With each step I have purpose, joy, and strength waiting for you. Every day I orchestrate events so riches are placed at your feet, purposes are placed in your heart and abundance is placed in your hands. These are my intentions for you – fullness of life, awakening of love, and incredible amounts of joy. It's going to be a good day, my child, a very good day for I wake up with you in mind.

_____

_____

_____

_____

_____

_____

_____

_____

_____

_____

_____

_____

_____

Psalm 136:1
¹ Give thanks to the Lord, for he is good.
His love endures forever.

Be Still Your Soul Today.

Be still your soul today. Rest in my presence, in my promises, and in the grace that is yours. You may feel overwhelmed by circumstances and even individuals around you, but I have designed you to live above the chaos. To purposefully allow your heart and mind to rest and let my peace meet you there. Rather than live in a state of overwhelmed torment, imagine yourself OVER the pressures of the day. You are called to be above and not beneath. From the very beginning I called you to reign and today is no different. This is your position and how I am preparing you for greater things that are still to come!

_____

_____

_____

_____

_____

_____

_____

_____

Deuteronomy 28:13
¹³ *The Lord will make you the head, not the tail.*
If you pay attention to the commands of the Lord your
God that I give you this day and carefully follow them,
you will always be at the top, never at the bottom.

I Have Prepared a Feast for You – A Feast with all the Fixings.

There's a feast I have for you. A table I set in the presence of your enemies. When you look around and see seemingly nothing, you look with eyes of the enemy, but you my child have MY eyes. Your eyes are filled with abundance, purpose, generosity, and joy. Through this view opportunity knocks at your door, divine appointments await your arrival, and wisdom is on a direct line to you from Heaven. Sit and dine with me today for I have prepared a feast with all the fixings.

_____

_____

_____

_____

_____

_____

_____

_____

_____

_____

Psalm 23:5

⁵ You prepare a table before me
in the presence of my enemies.
You anoint my head with oil;
my cup overflows.

I am Giving You the Keys.

I am giving you the keys. Keys to unlock the destiny I've prepared for you and keys to open doors of abundance. These keys reveal your potential and your greater purpose. Every day I set up divine relationships for you, with the intent to build upon your life. You have the power to change the course of history. Ask me for the keys and never stop trying the locks. You never know what doors might open!

_____

_____

_____

_____

_____

_____

_____

_____

_____

_____

_____

_____

_____

Matthew 16:19

19 *I will give you the keys of the kingdom of heaven; whatever you bind on earth will be*[a] *bound in heaven, and whatever you loose on earth will be*[b] *loosed in heaven."*

I am Blowing a Fresh Wind in Your Face Today.

I am blowing a fresh wind your way today. As you look at the trees you can see the bend and bow of each branch as it folds to the power of the breeze. In the same way, catch my spirit and allow yourself to move with these new winds of change. Just as the seasons pass by, you too will have seasons in which you must let go of the past to embrace the present. It's now where you must trust that I am producing new life all around you. So, enjoy today's breeze!

_____

_____

_____

_____

_____

_____

_____

_____

_____

_____

Psalm 121:7-8

⁷ The LORD will keep you from all harm —
he will watch over your life;
⁸ the LORD will watch over your coming and going
both now and forevermore.

I am Your Grip – Your Handle on Life.

I know it feels like there's a tornado in your soul, a wrestling in your spirit, and an anxiousness within. Inwardly you toss and turn and can't seem to find peace. Here in this moment I will come with what you need to give you your rest again. It may seem like you've lost true north, like you can get a grip, but I am your grip. I am your handle on life when it feels as if you're living in the eye of the storm. In reality the eye is the calm, the very center where I am leading you and causing you to rest.

_____
_____
_____
_____
_____
_____
_____
_____
_____
_____
_____

John 16:33

³³ *"I have told you these things, so that in me you*
may have peace. In this world you will have trouble.
But take heart! I have overcome the world."

I Come When You Least Expect It.

I come in unexpected places and in unexpected packages. There's no telling when and where I might show up. There's discovery in my presence, in finding where I reside, and where I want to move. At times it may seem like I am hiding but it's only for your benefit so that you would seek me with all of your heart. As you search you will find me. It's a promise I've given you, knowing I will never leave you. I can see you perfectly inside and out and understand all that burns within you. Keep on searching and looking for me in unexpected places and unexpected packages.

_____

_____

_____

_____

_____

_____

_____

_____

_____

_____

_____

_____

Jeremiah 29:13
13 You will seek me and find me when you seek me with all your heart.

Get Ready to Catch the Wind.

Get ready to take off. You're about to soar so get ready to spread your wings. There's a wind about to blow, a spirit you will catch to take you higher, further, and farther than you've ever gone before. You must look ahead, catch a glimpse of your destination, and expand your imagination. It's time to dream again, to think outside the box, and breakthrough the open doors in front of you. This release and acceleration is for your advancement. Your time is now and nothing and no one can hold you back.

_____

_____

_____

_____

_____

_____

_____

_____

_____

_____

_____

Isaiah 58:14
14 then you will find your joy in the LORD,
and I will cause you to ride in triumph on the heights of the land
and to feast on the inheritance of your father Jacob."
For the mouth of the LORD has spoken.

Your Joy Will Come in the Morning.

Disappointment will come, yes, but I will never leave you. My promises are true and always ready at your disposal. I see your hurt, pain, even the betrayal you've endured. Make no mistake your payment is coming, not in the world's form, but in a form, which brings blessing and abundance. When I was persecuted it was confirmation I was walking with my Father. Check in with me, discern where I am and how I am moving, and trust that better days are ahead, and your joy will surely come in the morning.

Psalm 30:5

⁵ *For his anger lasts only a moment,*
but his favor lasts a lifetime;
weeping may stay for the night,
but rejoicing comes in the morning.

You are Worth It and Deserve the World!

Y ou may want to run, hide, and lock yourself away from the world. You may think removing yourself from the situation is the best solution, but resist these lies which say, "You aren't good enough and aren't worth the time and effort of others." That is anything but the truth. You are precious, valuable, and worth moving mountains for. Hold your head up high, walk with a strut, and speak with confidence. You are worth it and deserve the world!

---

1 Peter 2:9

*⁹ But you are a chosen people, a royal priesthood,
a holy nation, God's special possession, that you
may declare the praises of him who called you out
of darkness into his wonderful light.*

Get Ready My Dear, for Your Time has Come.

You're about to take off; in fact, you're already on your way. This is the start of something great, something grand, and something huge. Tasks, appointments, and divine connections are being arranged and orchestrated as we speak. Your voice is being released and destiny is unfolding. You can't stop it or prevent it from happening. Just rest in my presence, sit at my feet, and listen to voice. Get ready for your time has come.

Job 42:2

² *"I know that you can do all things;*
no purpose of yours can be thwarted.

I Work All Things for Your Good.

Life is going to throw you curve balls. They are going to come from every different angle and from places and people you never expected. More than likely they will catch you off guard, and you'll have to move to avoid their sting. It's my spirit living within you that will alert you to act and turn in the right direction. It's my spirit guiding you every step of the way. At times it may seem like a detour or a setback, but I work all things for your good and I am the Master of turning lemons to lemonade. So, embrace the curve balls and I'll show you how to hit them out of the park!

_____

_____

_____

_____

_____

_____

_____

_____

_____

_____

_____

Proverbs 19:21

21 Many are the plans in a person's heart,
but it is the LORD's purpose that prevails.

It's Time to Have Fun!

It's time to have fun. Yes, you heard me right. Have FUN! What you do isn't important but the spirit behind it is. To laugh, smile and purposely pursue those people and activities that bring life, energy and joy. This is the fruit of my Kingdom and the foundation of my heartbeat. So dance like a child, sing like you're in the shower, and pursue those activities which bring life. It's time to have fun and yes, you most definitely have my permission!

Psalm 126:3

*³ The Lord has done great things for us,
and we are filled with joy.*

When It's Time to Let Go – Let Go.

Y ou're tired, worn out, and exhausted. In your toil you must remember, I haven't called you to the many but the few. I haven't called you to the masses but to a unique set of people and tasks which you are divinely set apart for. You can't do it all, and you can't please everyone. Look at where you're overloaded and where I want to release your burdens. Look to where I haven't called you and step out of this responsibility. My burden is light, and I will never ask you to carry more than you can handle. If it's time to let go... you'll know.

_____

_____

_____

_____

_____

_____

_____

_____

_____

_____

_____

_____

Job 17:9
⁹ Nevertheless, the righteous will hold to their ways,
and those with clean hands will grow stronger.

Keep Going and Keep Moving.

Keep going and keep moving. Sometimes there's no map and no direction and it seems like you are walking in circles. But I haven't called you to know all the details and don't expect you to have every inch meticulously planned out. I've called you to follow my voice, to trust me as your roadmap, and in this pursuit, and you'll never miss a beat. There's no stopping you with me as your guide! So keep going and keep moving!

_____

_____

_____

_____

_____

_____

_____

_____

_____

_____

Proverbs 4:25-27

²⁵ Let your eyes look straight ahead;
fix your gaze directly before you.
²⁶ Give careful thought to the[a] paths for your feet
and be steadfast in all your ways.
²⁷ Do not turn to the right or the left;
keep your foot from evil.

It's the Start of a Fresh Beginning.

With the dawn of a new day is the start of a fresh beginning. Tomorrow is gone. Don't dwell on it and do not live in it like it is still the present. The mistakes or perceived mistakes of yesterday don't hold you back. You begin again and awake without the chains of yesterday tying you down. Remember your dreams and remember my promises over you. It's time run without restraint, dance without limits, and soar beyond the heights. No longer will the past predict your future, but your future will be created with each step you take!

_____

_____

_____

_____

_____

_____

_____

_____

_____

_____

_____

_____

Psalm 32:8

8 *I will instruct you and teach you in the way you should go;*
I will counsel you with my loving eye on you.

I am Setting You Up for More!

Y ou think you've missed it. Your life has flashed before your eyes, and you sense opportunities and divine opportunities have passed you by. This couldn't be farther from the truth. Instead they are waiting at your door, ready for you to greet them and say, "Greetings!" Welcome them with open arms and approach them with confidence knowing that I have readied you for these appointments. You haven't missed anything. In fact, I am setting you up for more!

_____

_____

_____

_____

_____

_____

_____

_____

_____

_____

_____

_____

_____

_____

_____

1 Corinthians 16:13
¹³ *Be on your guard; stand firm in the faith;*
be courageous; be strong.

Welcome This Day with Anticipation!

Every day I invite you to welcome the day with anticipation. What you expect will show up at your door. Let your eyes be filled with hope, faith and love because this is what I have for you. You can look for it, seek it, and indeed you will find it. Abundance awaits you and there is nothing I withhold from you. Get giddy, get excited and prepare for what's to come – there are good things ahead!

Proverbs 17:22

²² A cheerful heart is good medicine,
but a crushed spirit dries up the bones.

As Sure as the Sun Rises are My Promises True for You.

As sure as the sun rises are my promises true for you. They greet you each morning with a smile that affirms who you are and the destiny I have for you. I don't carry over the cares of yesterday into today, but I look at your life and the road ahead with nothing but eyes of anticipation on how I plan to bless you and pour out my abundance to you. Like a Father who desires the best for His children, I desire every one of your steps to be met with my goodness and grace.

_____

_____

_____

_____

_____

_____

_____

_____

_____

_____

_____

Psalm 121:1-2

¹ I lift up my eyes to the mountains —
where does my help come from?
² My help comes from the LORD,
the Maker of heaven and earth.

327

Refocus, Re-engage and Re-direct to Me.

Refocus and re-engage your mind to where I am moving. Stop, listen, and re-direct your attention to me. If you seek me, you will find me. If you're looking for answers, I have the solution. If you're needing wisdom, I have what you need. Never will you be in need. I am here, ready to meet you right where you are. So, refocus today and redirect your thoughts to me. As you turn your focus to me, your heart will quickly follow.

_____

_____

_____

_____

_____

_____

_____

_____

_____

_____

John 14:26-27

26 But the Advocate, the Holy Spirit, whom the Father will send in my name, will teach you all things and will remind you of everything I have said to you. 27 Peace I leave with you; my peace I give you. I do not give to you as the world gives. Do not let your hearts be troubled and do not be afraid.

I Will Show You, I Will Meet You & I Will Greet You Here.

It's time to dive into a new beginning and run without restraint. It's time to believe the absolute best because that's what I have for you. As you look ahead, look with me, and let me show you how to move and where with whom. The enemy wants you distracted with this and that and seemingly "good things", but I want you to soar. Dial into me, dial into my voice and focus on me. I will show you. I will meet you here and everywhere.

_____

_____

_____

_____

_____

_____

_____

_____

_____

_____

Psalm 121:5-6

⁵ *The LORD watches over you—*
the LORD is your shade at your right hand;
⁶ *the sun will not harm you by day,*
nor the moon by night.

November
Devotional

Remember How I Have Been Faithful to You.

Remember this day how I have been faithful to you. I provide all you need, and I extend my blessing time and time again. My faithfulness will never leave you. If doubt, worry, and fear begin to plague your mind kick them to the curb because that is not your true reality. Remind yourself again and again. Write it on your mirror, hang a note on your fridge, and fill your life with messages that will keep my goodness in the forefront. Remembering my faithfulness is the key that unlocks gratitude and a heart of contentment. Remember because I never forget.

_____

_____

_____

_____

_____

_____

_____

_____

_____

_____

_____

Matthew 28:20

[20] *and teaching them to obey everything I have commanded you. And surely, I am with you always, to the very end of the age."*

Right Now is Where I've Called You to Live.

Right now is where I've called you to live. Right now I have provisions for you. Right now divine relationships are being set to come your way. The past is the past. You don't live there anymore, and the future isn't guaranteed. Right now I speak to your heart and command forth your destiny. In the present is where you experience the fullness of life, I have promised you. Stop, enjoy this moment and feast on my presence. Right now is what I am giving you, and where I have the best for you.

_____

_____

_____

_____

_____

_____

_____

_____

_____

_____

Psalm 86:17

17 Give me a sign of your goodness,
that my enemies may see it and be put to shame,
for you, LORD, have helped me and comforted me.

In the Taking Away is Where I am Able to Come and Fill.

Take time today to de-clutter your life. Cut the fat, trim the muck and get rid of the unwanted. My desire is that your mind would be clear from the unnecessary noise and chaos so that your heart can live in perfect peace. Look for space today to clear your schedule, clear your desk, and dispose of what is unnecessary. In the taking away is where I am able to come and fill. So clear the way and make room for more!

_____

_____

_____

_____

_____

_____

_____

_____

_____

_____

Exodus 34:5-6

⁵ Then the LORD came down in the cloud and stood there with him and proclaimed his name, the LORD. ⁶ And he passed in front of Moses, proclaiming, "The LORD, the LORD, the compassionate and gracious God, slow to anger, abounding in love and faithfulness.

Worry Gets You Nowhere.

Worry gets you nowhere. It literally stops you in your tracks, a paralyzing force. The torment in your mind keeps your heart from engaging with the person in front of you. Your head spins, your heart races, and you can't help but anticipate the worst. A word from my heart is what you need to hear, and then the thoughts in your mind will shift and the atmosphere around you will adjust. Look, listen, and rest long enough so that my whispers will resound like a shout. Then worry will no longer be your anchor but hope will be your song.

_____

_____

_____

_____

_____

_____

_____

_____

_____

_____

_____

_____

Psalm 119:76
76 May your unfailing love be my comfort,
according to your promise to your servant.

Keep Going – There's Light Up Ahead.

Don't give up. At just the right time you will see the fruits of your labor. Just before your moment of breakthrough lies the greatest tension, so don't quit now. Walk forward, walk slowly if you must, but keep walking. Don't look back but only forward for even the slightest movement in the wrong direction delays your progress. Keep your eyes ahead, keep your gaze fixed on the prize, and do not abandon your goals. Keep believing; keep hoping, and soon you'll see the light.

_____

_____

_____

_____

_____

Psalm 103:1-5

¹ Praise the LORD, my soul;
all my inmost being, praise his holy name.
² Praise the LORD, my soul,
and forget not all his benefits –
³ who forgives all your sins
and heals all your diseases,
⁴ who redeems your life from the pit
and crowns you with love and compassion,
⁵ who satisfies your desires with good things
so that your youth is renewed like the eagle's.

Keep Fighting for Those You Love.

Today remember to fight for relationships. To forgive, let go of hurt, walk in love, and keep striving to keep the peace. Connection is the core of who you are. It's how I designed you to be. Without love, without a relationship with Me and the people around you, what else is there? This is why I've made you - to live with each other in such a way that nothing would come against you and nothing would separate you from me and from each other. Fight today for love. Fight today to keep the unity. There's nothing more important - no task or schedule more important than a renewed connection with the ones you love.

_____

_____

_____

_____

_____

_____

_____

_____

_____

Hebrews 10:24-25

24 And let us consider how we may spur one another on toward love and good deeds, 25 not giving up meeting together, as some are in the habit of doing, but encouraging one another and all the more as you see the Day approaching.

Stop Rushing & Choose to Go at My Pace.

With so much to do and so many people to engage with, it can be easy to forget about me as you quickly find yourself on the hamster wheel of life. In these times it's all the more important to stop, breathe and listen. To get off the spinning wheel and choose to go at my pace. I am not rushed, hurried, or running franticly. I am attentive to my environment, focused on the current task, and dialed to you. This too should be your posture and the pace I desire for you. You CAN get off the rat race of life. It's simply a choice!

_____

_____

_____

_____

_____

_____

_____

_____

_____

_____

Psalm 107:8-9

[8] *Let them give thanks to the LORD for his unfailing love*
and his wonderful deeds for mankind,
[9] *for he satisfies the thirsty*
and fills the hungry with good things.

Gaze Higher at the Bigger Picture.

What's the big picture I have called you to? Where do you want to be in 5, 10, or 50 years from now? The daily grind you find yourself in is projecting you towards a greater goal, and you're picking up steam with every passing day. Look ahead and look beyond what currently meets your eye and gaze to the future. Don't let yourself get bogged down in daily tasks and forget the greater prize. Focus on my long-term plans and allow this vision to fuel your days and ignite your week.

_____
_____
_____
_____
_____
_____
_____
_____
_____
_____
_____
_____
_____
_____

Luke 9:62

*⁶²Jesus replied, "No one who puts a hand to the plow
and looks back is fit for service in the kingdom of God."*

Recall My Faithfulness that I May Meet You Again.

To forget my blessings towards you is to forget that I have always provided your every need. Recall my faithfulness so doubt, fear, and worry will be pushed away. In meditating on what I've done your faith will be restored, your hope will be renewed, and your love will increase. Remember today and every day because it's here, dwelling on my goodness, that I come and meet you once again.

_____

_____

_____

_____

_____

_____

_____

_____

_____

_____

Deuteronomy 7:9

9 Know therefore that the LORD your God is God;
he is the faithful God, keeping his covenant of love
to a thousand generations of those who love
him and keep his commandments.

I am Already There Waiting for You to Show Up.

With every step forward you're walking in purpose. With every step forward, you're making your mark. With every step forward, you move toward your destiny. I see your impact and influence. Passion begins to burst through. You're making progress and you're gaining clarity. With every step forward, I am giving you a new and fresh perspective and most importantly with every step forward, I am already there waiting for your presence!

_____

_____

_____

_____

_____

_____

_____

_____

_____

_____

_____

_____

Psalm 81:10
[10] I am the LORD your God,
who brought you up out of Egypt.
Open wide your mouth and I will fill it.

342

Cut Back so I Can Fill You Once Again.

I am a God of abundance, a Father that seeks to add upon your life and bless you in every way. But just as important as the provisions I bring you is the space needed to pour out those blessings. It may be time to dial back in order to make room for what I am preparing for you. It may be time to clear out your desk, clean out your closet and empty your junk drawer. In both the physical and the spiritual a clearing out is necessary. Let go of what's collecting dust so you can invite new and fresh provisions into your life. It may seem empty and bare but in reality, you're preparing for the abundance that is about to fill this space once again.

_____

_____

_____

_____

_____

_____

_____

Deuteronomy 11:13-14

[13] So if you faithfully obey the commands I am giving you today — to love the LORD, your God and to serve him with all your heart and with all your soul — [14] then I will send rain on your land in its season, both autumn and spring rains, so that you may gather in your grain, new wine and olive oil.

Keep an Open Mind. I am Not Always What You Expect.

Keep an open mind. I am not always as you expect. I don't always show up in a pretty little box with everything in its place. Proper, formal, and neat isn't often the way I operate. I am in the mess, in the chaos, and in the impossible. There are no limits on me, no barriers around me, and no structure that's placed over me. Keep your mind open, your heart searching, and your spirit steadfast on me because you just might be surprised where and when I show up!

_____

_____

_____

_____

_____

_____

_____

_____

_____

_____

_____

1 Samuel 12:24

²⁴ *But be sure to fear the LORD and serve him faithfully with all your heart; consider what great things he has done for you.*

344

Breathe. Keep Breathing and then Breathe Again.

Breathe. Just Breathe. In and out, fully relaxing every inch of your body. There's no rush, no hurry, and nothing you are missing. Stop, rest, and enjoy this moment. Say a prayer of thankfulness, extend a word of gratitude, and allow your heart to transition to a peaceful state. Breathe. Keep breathing. Sometimes deep, sometimes slow. There's no rush. It's in the simple things of life where I reside and where I am found. Enjoy the depth and breadth of today. Sometimes it's as easy as that.

Ezekiel 18:9

9 He follows my decrees
and faithfully keeps my laws.
That man is righteous;
he will surely live,
declares the Sovereign LORD.

Look Out, Walk Upright and Watch How I Provide.

How's your walk today? Are your steps filled with integrity? Are they cemented in love? Are they seasoned with truth? What you sow is what you'll reap. This is a principle in my Kingdom and an aspect of who I am. To walk in such a way where your focus is outward, and your hand is ready to give is the quickest way to ensure I'll take care of you. Look outward, walk upright, and watch how I'll provide.

Galatians 6:7-8

*7 Do not be deceived: God cannot be mocked.
A man reaps what he sows. 8 Whoever sows to please
their flesh, from the flesh will reap destruction;
whoever sows to please the Spirit, from the
Spirit will reap eternal life.*

346

Don't Go Through the Motions Today.

Don't go through the motions like there are no other options. I haven't made you to run frantically through life and I haven't designed you to spin tirelessly on the hamster wheel. Every day I have surprises for you. Each day I greet you with a smile affirming my delight over you. Consciously remove yourself from lifeless tasks and invite me into each moment. In every invitation I meet you there and begin to unfold a new pattern and rhythm for the day. A new routine that brings you joy and love and will keep you from just checking boxes!

_____

_____

_____

_____

_____

_____

_____

_____

_____

_____

_____

Hebrews 10:35-36

[35] *So do not throw away your confidence; it will be richly rewarded.*
[36] *You need to persevere so that when you have done the will of God, you will receive what he has promised.*

Keep Walking, Keep Going, and Don't Look Back!

Keep walking, keep going. Keep moving forward and don't look back. Keep your eyes outward, not inward and enjoy each moment of the day because a new season is coming, and it won't look like where you've been. The road ahead may seem hard and completely unfamiliar and that's ok. Listen for my voice in this season, look for my presence to manifest in new ways and watch as I am waiting around each corner. There are new things ahead and new ways I want to bless you.

_____

_____

_____

_____

_____

_____

_____

_____

_____

_____

_____

Isaiah 26:4

⁴ *Trust in the LORD forever,*
for the LORD, the LORD himself, is the Rock eternal.

Live Above Your Feelings Today – They Don't Rule You!

Having a rough day? Don't feel like doing anything or being around anyone? Just do the opposite of what you feel. Call a friend. Declare out loud how wonderful, beautiful, smart and talented you are. Bake your neighbor brownies. Go out of your way to do a friend a favor. Call a family member and let them know you appreciate them. Take a bubble bath. Take a nap. See if doing the opposite of how you feel will turn the tide on your day. You are not ruled by your negative feelings – live above them today and you'll be the one rewarded.

_____

_____

_____

_____

_____

_____

_____

_____

_____

_____

John 14:1

[1] *"Do not let your hearts be troubled.*
You believe in God; believe also in me.

If You Search for Me, You Will Find Me.

If you search for me, you will find me. If you look for me with all your heart, mind, and soul I'll be there waiting. Every day is a treasure where I have gifts, wisdom, and promises for you around every turn. Get out your spyglasses, put on your coat of adventure, and begin to navigate the waters of my heart. I eagerly look for those who are looking for me. My heart gravitates towards the hungry, faithful, and willing. Dive in and discover the surprises that I have hidden for you alone.

_____

_____

_____

_____

_____

_____

_____

_____

_____

_____

_____

Psalm 86:2-3

² Guard my life, for I am faithful to you;
save your servant who trusts in you.
You are my God; ³ have mercy on me, Lord,
for I call to you all day long.

Get Ready to Paint the Town!

Paint a new color on the day. Ask me for a different shade, a new perspective, and fresh coat upon your life. I don't operate from old patterns and old ways. Instead I continue to create exciting new accents on your life. Keep in step with me, and you'll see how I can brighten a room and add life to your day. If you're staring at an old shade on the color palette, now's the time to ask me for an upgrade. I have fresh colors I want to drop into your life and various shades I want to show you. It's a new day, a new dawn, so get ready to paint the town!

Matthew 25:21

[21] *"His master replied, 'Well done, good and faithful servant! You have been faithful with a few things; I will put you in charge of many things. Come and share your master's happiness!'*

Declare Your Boundaries – They are for Your Good!

Boundaries are everywhere you look. The ocean hits the shore, the river separates the valley, and the lake meets the land. I've designed the earth this way and I've designed you in the same. Yes and no are words that carry power. They declare what's ok and what's not ok. You decide whom you let in and at what level they have access to your heart and life. You have ownership and you have control. Declare your boundaries because I've created them and intended them for your good!

_____

_____

_____

_____

_____

_____

_____

_____

_____

_____

Psalm 101:6

⁶ My eyes will be on the faithful in the land,
that they may dwell with me;
the one whose walk is blameless
will minister to me.

Soak Up each Moment,
It's Here Where I am.

If you're caught up in the moment, then you're right where I am. Here, now, present, and ready to meet you. I am what you need, I have what you desire, and I will fulfill every provision. To be found in the moment is to take advantage of everything and everyone I have placed around you. Don't rush from task to task and don't scurry from appointment to appointment. Instead find me steady, resting, and fully present in the moments of everyday. Soak up each moment, for it's here where I am.

_____

_____

_____

_____

_____

_____

_____

_____

Luke 12:42-44

42 The Lord answered, "Who then is the faithful and wise manager, whom the master puts in charge of his servants to give them their food allowance at the proper time? 43 It will be good for that servant whom the master finds doing so when he returns. 44 Truly I tell you, he will put him in charge of all his possessions.

I See You, Inside and Out, I See You.

I see you today. I see where you've been, where you're going, and how you will get there. I SEE you. Inside and out I have crafted you perfectly. Your personality, your gifts, your talents, and your unique nature. I saw you then, and I see you now. All your days I planned before you – to walk in my goodness and to be found in my grace. I see you without fault each and every day. Nothing is hidden, and nothing is missed. I see you perfectly.

_____

_____

_____

_____

_____

_____

_____

_____

_____

_____

_____

_____

John 7:37-38

37 On the last and greatest day of the festival, Jesus stood and said in a loud voice, "Let anyone who is thirsty come to me and drink. 38 Whoever believes in me, as Scripture has said, rivers of living water will flow from within them."

Don't Stop Believing and Never Stop Dreaming.

Don't stop believing. Never stop dreaming. I live in the impossible. I reside in the "could never be" of life. When you feel your stomach start to churn, the doubts begin to flood in and your mind plagued with questions, this is where I am moving and where I am ready to speak. Flush out the doubt, fear, and worry and step forward in confidence. Don't stop believing and keep on dreaming because you never know when I am about to breakthrough!

_____

_____

_____

_____

_____

_____

_____

_____

_____

_____

Mark 10:51-52

51 *"What do you want me to do for you?" Jesus asked him. The blind man said, "Rabbi, I want to see."*
52 *"Go," said Jesus, "your faith has healed you." Immediately he received his sight and followed Jesus along the road.*

What's Your One Thing Today?

When your head is spinning, and you can't seem to get any direction use this opportunity to focus on one thing. Yes, just one thing. Ask me what your "one thing" should be! Then dial in, trusting that I'll help you take care of the rest. Let go of the expectations that are on your shoulders, let go of the unnecessary weights you carry and instead allow your heart, soul and mind to fully enter into your ONE thing!

_____

_____

_____

_____

_____

_____

_____

_____

_____

_____

_____

_____

Mark 11:24

24 Therefore I tell you, whatever you ask for in prayer, believe that you have received it, and it will be yours.

If You're Ready for Help, I am Ready to Give It.

D o you need help? Are you in need of wisdom and guidance? This is my specialty and what I love to freely give. Are you wondering, waiting, and unsure if you should take action or sit back in silence? These are the situations I love to help you with. I give Fatherly advice that isn't marked with guilt, manipulation or condemnation but filled with faith, hope and love. The answers I give you will allow you to walk in peace knowing that you're moving in the right direction. If you're ready for help, I am ready to provide my wisdom.

_____

_____

_____

_____

_____

_____

_____

2 Corinthians 5:6-8
*⁶ Therefore we are always confident and know that
as long as we are at home in the body we are away from the Lord. ⁷
For we live by faith, not by sight. ⁸ We are confident, I say,
and would prefer to be away from the body and
at home with the Lord.*

You're Gaining Momentum!

You're gaining momentum! Everyday you're working towards a larger goal. With your sight on the horizon you must keep going. You have come too far to give up now. There's still opportunity in front of you and divine appointments I have set for you. Trust that what I have been building in you will soon manifest outside of you. You will soon see the fruits of your daily grind as your goals are realized.

_____

_____

_____

_____

_____

_____

_____

_____

_____

_____

_____

_____

1 Thessalonians 1:3
*³ We remember before our God and Father your
work produced by faith, your labor prompted by love,
and your endurance inspired by hope in our Lord Jesus Christ.*

Ask, Seek, and Knock for the Wisdom You Need Today.

You're tired, you're weary and you need a break, yet your spirit says to keep going, keep moving and don't give up. Rather than focusing on all the tasks and appointments in front of you, just do the next thing you know to do. Ask me what's most important, ask me what demands your attention, and wait for my response. It might be a nap, it might be extra time with your kids, it might be tidying up the garage, or it might be that extra bit of work. I won't overwhelm you; I won't spread you too thin. Ask, seek and knock for the wisdom you need today and trust I will surely answer.

_____

_____

_____

_____

_____

_____

_____

_____

Ephesians 6:16-17

*16 In addition to all this, take up the shield of faith,
with which you can extinguish all the flaming arrows
of the evil one. 17 Take the helmet of salvation and the
sword of the Spirit, which is the word of God.*

Put on Your Oxygen Mask First.

Today I give you permission to put your oxygen mask on first. To dial into your lifelines and commit to those people and tasks which bring you energy and life. Make time and space for you today, saying no or not yet to the commitments that suck you dry. My desire for you is a healthy pursuit of the purposes and passions so that you can live from a place of peace, contentment and love. Today I give you permission to focus on you and breathe in deep to *your* oxygen mask.

2 Corinthians 1:24
24 Not that we lord it over your faith, but we work with you for your joy; because it is by faith you stand firm.

I Came to Set You Free.

One word and everything changes. All it takes is a single thought and the light bulb clicks on. I didn't come here to give you a complicated plan for how to live. I came to set you free. One glance at Jesus and you'll be changed; one message from Him and you'll walk in freedom. Don't go out looking for a more complicated solution. Don't go searching for a routine that will weigh you down. I'll give you answers, I'll give you what you need, because I AM the solution, I AM the answer, and I AM what you need.

_____

_____

_____

_____

_____

_____

_____

_____

_____

_____

_____

1 Corinthians 2:4-5

*⁴ My message and my preaching were not with wise
and persuasive words, but with a demonstration of the
Spirit's power, ⁵ so that your faith might not rest on
human wisdom, but on God's power.*

Run Wildly After the Purposes in Your Heart!

Determine what you want to do and begin. I'll step in if you venture the wrong way, I'll move in front of you if you take a detour, and I'll redirect you if you get off base. At the start of creation, I also created you and fashioned your unique personality, gifts and talents, and now you get to run with them. I am not a Father who controls and micromanages your every move. Instead I release you, to run wildly after the purposes and passions which ignite your heart!

_____

_____

_____

_____

_____

_____

_____

_____

2 Timothy 4:7-8

*7 I have fought the good fight, I have finished the race,
I have kept the faith. 8 Now there is in store for me the
crown of righteousness, which the Lord, the righteous Judge,
will award to me on that day — and not only to me, but
also to all who have longed for his appearing.*

December
Devotional

It All Begins with a Tidying of the Heart.

Sometimes what we need is a tidying of the heart. A moment, a day, a week, a month to have the space to dial back and allow Him to cleanse your heart. There is yuck and junk which needs to be purged. There is unnecessary crud which He won't allow to weigh us down anymore. Together you detach from what must no longer hold you back and finally loosen your grip on what you've been holding onto. With the distractions removed, He's giving you order, straightening your priorities and showing you again where true life and love come. He's re-ordering you back to its original design and it all begins with a tidying of the heart.

_____

_____

_____

_____

_____

_____

_____

_____

_____

_____

_____

Proverbs 21:21

²¹ *Whoever pursues righteousness and love*
finds life, prosperity and honor.

Good Morning My Friend!

Good morning my friend, for it is right to call you my friend. I don't talk to you like a child, although you are my child. I don't look at you like you're my puppet on a string. I see you as friend, companion and confidant. It's a friend you tell your secrets, your goals, your dreams, and you trust them with your life. I long to hear your heart, listen to your joys, struggles, and pains, and look forward to every moment together. So see me as a friend today because that is surely how I see you.

_____

_____

_____

_____

_____

_____

_____

_____

_____

_____

_____

_____

John 15:13

[13] *Greater love has no one than this: to lay down one's life for one's friends.*

I am Bigger Today Than Your Circumstances.

I am bigger today than your circumstances. I am larger today than your problems. When I look at your life, I don't see chaos and confusion, I see my hand securely over you, guiding you and leading you forward. Worry, doubt, and fear are not the cloak you wear. Faith, hope and love are the armor I give you. I am the answer to your problem and the wisdom to your question. I am bigger than what confronts you.

_____

_____

_____

_____

_____

_____

_____

_____

_____

_____

2 Corinthians 9:7

⁷ Each of you should give what you have decided
in your heart to give, not reluctantly or under
compulsion, for God loves a cheerful giver.

Be Sure to Pick from the Fruit of My Tree Today.

Look at the fruit in your life. Is it peaceful, joyful, and full of love and grace? Or is it filled with confusion, fear and heaviness? When you notice the fruit, you'll notice where I am headed and where I am directing you. This is my calling card and how you'll see it's me. My spirit is power, love, self-control and a sound mind. I awaken; I enlighten and draw you closer to others and myself. This is who I am. What's the fruit you're seeing, experiencing, and living? Only pick what is good and only take what I have provided.

_____

_____

_____

_____

_____

_____

_____

_____

_____

_____

_____

_____

Ephesians 4:32

³² *Be kind and compassionate to one another,*
forgiving each other, just as in Christ God forgave you.

Listen, Wait, and Listen Today.

Before you speak, before you act, before you move, listen. Listen to my voice. There are things I want to tell you, promises I want to give you, and a direction I want to show you. When you listen you begin to understand, you begin to see the world around you clearly, and you can position yourself correctly. Listen, wait and listen. Have patience and trust that I'll say just what you need to hear, just when you need to hear it.

_____

_____

_____

_____

_____

_____

_____

_____

_____

_____

_____

_____

Psalm 46:10

10 He says, "Be still, and know that I am God;
I will be exalted among the nations,
I will be exalted in the earth."

I am Ready to Take You Higher.

Just as our four seasons change every few months, so does life. With change comes anticipation, excitement, dread, nervous tension and everything in between. You can't predict the future or perfectly plan every moment but with hope await what lies ahead. Sometimes you know what's coming and other times you hold your breath for every unknown. Entering into a new transition means I've seen where you've been, understand where you're going and am ready to take you to the next level!

Psalm 20:4
*⁴ May he give you the desire of your heart
and make all your plans succeed.*

The Grass is Both Green and Growing.

Don't get caught in the trap of looking at the life of your friends, family or the neighbor next door thinking they're further ahead than you. It seems the grass is always greener and maybe in some sense it is but now you're playing with fire. To compare your life to another is to wish away your own and so very quickly you'll find yourself further away from happiness and contentment than you ever thought possible. Ask me for a clear picture of your life today, the true perspective of where you are, and you'll start to see your grass is both green and growing!

_____

_____

_____

_____

_____

_____

_____

_____

_____

_____

Psalm 56:3-4

3 When I am afraid, I put my trust in you.
4 In God, whose word I praise —
in God I trust and am not afraid.
What can mere mortals do to me?

Your Heart is a Treasure.
Guard it with Your Life.

Your heart is a treasure - full of gold, jewels, amazing gifts, talents, and wisdom. Guard this treasure with your life. Don't let just anyone come and rob your valuable treasures. You are worth more than that. Protect what I've given you and the uniqueness in how I've made you. Be wise with whom you share your gold understanding how precious each piece is. Guard your heart as if your life depends on it because in actuality it does.

Psalm 112:1

¹ Praise the LORD.
Blessed are those who fear the LORD,
who find great delight in his commands.

I am the Way, the Truth and the Life.

Every day you are bombarded with information. There are billboards, commercials, work discussions, and family conversations. It can be overwhelming at times and leave you feeling exhausted even before the weekend begins. Remember today that I am the way, the truth and the life and the one information source you can always depend on. Check in with me and confirm the details. I won't drown you but will give you the information you need when you need it!

_____

_____

_____

_____

_____

_____

_____

_____

_____

_____

_____

Job 1:21
21 *"Naked I came from my mother's womb,*
and naked I will depart.
The Lord gave and the Lord has taken away;
may the name of the Lord be praised."

You Can Always Trust
I am Right Here Waiting.

In a second everything can change. In a day your world can be turned upside down so be thankful, remain grateful, and grab onto each moment. I've designed this life to be enjoyed and embraced so as the change comes you can trust I am right there with you. Even when life can't be explained I'll meet you in that moment and lavish on you my goodness and grace. Shout out your list of gratitude today, declare boldly your heart of thankfulness because you never know what's around the corner, but you'll always know, and you can trust that I am right there waiting.

_____

_____

_____

_____

_____

_____

_____

_____

_____

_____

Psalm 103:17

17 But from everlasting to everlasting
the LORD's love is with those who fear him,
and his righteousness with their children's children.

I Have Your Heart and I Hold It Close.

Know today that I have your heart and I hold it close. My desire is to help you protect it, guard it, letting in what is good and keeping out the bad. From here passion, truth and abundant love will flow. From here wisdom, grace, and peace will pour out. From here desire, intrigue, and creativity will burst forth. From the inside out I see your heart, every piece, every inch, every true desire – and hold it close.

Psalm 115:11

11 *You who fear him, trust in the LORD –*
he is their help and shield.

375

You are Creative – Absolutely Creative!

You're creative. Absolutely you're creative. It doesn't mean you love to draw, paint or write (although you might). It means that from the inside out you have fresh ideas, solutions, and wisdom that are being birthed every day. It means new plans continually fill up your heart, soul, and mind. Yes, you are creative because you were made by The Creator. Allow yourself to think outside the box because in reality the box doesn't even exist but only my spirit, which helps you create beyond your wildest imagination!

_____

_____

_____

_____

_____

_____

_____

_____

_____

Isaiah 40:28

²⁸ Do you not know?
Have you not heard?
The LORD is the everlasting God,
the Creator of the ends of the earth.
He will not grow tired or weary,
and his understanding no one can fathom.

You are in a Season of Preparation!

Y ou think you're in a season of waiting when in actuality you are in a season of preparation. There are no stagnant seasons, no seasons in which I put you in a holding pattern. If you think life seems slow, then you can trust I am growing you beneath the surface and pushing your foundation further into the ground. This is for your lifelong and your lifelong growth so that when the storms come or the roads gets rocky, you'll be ready, you'll be prepared, and you'll be equipped with what you need to move ahead.

_____

_____

_____

_____

_____

_____

_____

_____

_____

_____

_____

Psalm 118:24

24 The LORD has done it this very day;
let us rejoice today and be glad.

Take Care of YOU – Every Day!

Take care of yourself for in doing so you take care of me. You house my presence, and your very being is a vessel which I flow through. Take naps, long walks, and eat well, and don't forget to enjoy the pleasures of life, but don't indulge in that which does not benefit you. See your body as a beautiful gift from me that is to be nurtured and valued. Connect with me on how I made you and I promise together we'll take care of you!

_____

_____

_____

_____

_____

_____

_____

_____

_____

_____

_____

2 Chronicles 7:14
¹⁴ if my people, who are called by my name,
will humble themselves and pray and seek my face
and turn from their wicked ways, then I will hear from heaven,
and I will forgive their sin and will heal their land.

I am Setting You Up for Life.

I am setting you up for life. Each and every day I am placing you in a position for success. Each conversation, each task and each encounter are divine appointments by me, your Father. I have your best interest in mind. I see the desires of your heart and I look for opportunities to bless you, provide for you, and show my goodness to you. When you look back wondering what that was about, or you look forward wondering how life will fall into place, know that I see it all and am positioning you each and every day for true success.

Romans 8:17-19

17 Now if we are children, then we are heirs—heirs of God and co-heirs with Christ, if indeed we share in his sufferings in order that we may also share in his glory. 18 I consider that our present sufferings are not worth comparing with the glory that will be revealed in us. 19 For the creation waits in eager expectation for the children of God to be revealed.

Stay Poised & Remain Focused.

Stay poised and remain focused on what's important and what truly matters. Take down your guard, take down your shield and dial into my heart and voice. Don't get caught up in the judgements, the rumors and the endless opinions. Stay after the truth, and remain calm, cool and collected. Nothing good every came from an anger outburst, and nothing productive ever came from a split-second burst of frustration. Stop, breathe, reflect, and assume the best about everyone around you. There's wisdom in waiting and understanding in patience. Let your nerves settle and let my peace enter in.

Micah 6:8

8 He has shown you, O mortal, what is good.
And what does the Lord require of you?
To act justly and to love mercy
and to walk humbly with your God.

How You Think is How You Act.

How you think is how you act. Focus your thoughts on what's good, what's hopeful. Turn your attention to gratitude and stay in a place of thankfulness. Look for me in the small things and big things. Allow your expectation to soar higher and watch what I do. Your mind carries power, love and peace. This is who you are and the daily stance you hold. How you think is how you act, so let me come and fill your thoughts today so Godly actions will surely follow!

_____

_____

_____

_____

_____

_____

_____

_____

_____

_____

_____

_____

Romans 12:2

² Do not conform to the pattern of this world but be transformed by the renewing of your mind. Then you will be able to test and approve what God's will is – his good, pleasing and perfect will.

I Do Not With hold Good from You!

I'll send you opportunities. I'll grant you provisions. I see what's ahead and I plan for your best. I am the great I am, and nothing do I withhold from you whom I love. Yes, you have a part to play, steps to take and tasks to complete. Stay diligent and focused on your every assignment trusting I will take care of the rest. I am the great I am, and no good thing do I withhold from you. Remember this always and keep this, my promise to you, securely in your heart!

_____

_____

_____

_____

_____

_____

_____

_____

_____

_____

_____

_____

James 3:13

¹³ *Who is wise and understanding among you?*
Let them show it by their good life, by deeds done
in the humility that comes from wisdom.

Come to Me with the Highs and Lows.

Ask me those questions. Tell me your frustrations. Come to me with the highs and the lows and everything in between. I am not afraid of your emotions. I am not scared of your anger, hurt, jealously, or even rage. I only desire to connect with you in the realness of your reality. It's then in your honesty and rawness that I am able to meet your need and give you a fresh, new and clear perspective. So tell me it all, and never stop sharing your true, real feelings. It's here where I connect with you and it's the connection with you that I desire.

Revelation 22:17

*17 The Spirit and the bride say, "Come!" And let the one
who hears say, "Come!" Let the one who is thirsty come;
and let the one who wishes take the free gift of the water of life.*

You're Not a Quitter.

Y ou're not a quitter. That's not in your DNA. You don't give up, you don't throw in the towel – that's NOT who you are. That is NOT how I created you. You are strong, creative, a problem-solver, and full of wisdom and insight. It might be time to change what you're doing or stop that habit as the season has ended. It's ok to alter your course but know that you have it in you to not give up, to keep fighting, and keep your focus today!

_____

_____

_____

_____

_____

_____

_____

_____

_____

_____

_____

Numbers 23:19
¹⁹ God is not human, that he should lie,
not a human being, that he should change his mind.
Does he speak and then not act?
Does he promise and not fulfill?

Laugh Today and Laugh Often.

Laugh often, frequently, understanding that there's joy around every corner. Maybe you don't feel like laughing and that's ok, but don't forget I am often found in the smiles. This is where life is birthed, and a good deep chuckle is always good for the soul. Even if you don't feel like smiling, just think of the last thing that made you truly happy and quickly you'll see joy fill your heart and love fill your soul. Laugh today and laugh often.

_____

_____

_____

_____

_____

_____

_____

_____

_____

_____

_____

_____

Philippians 1:3

3 I thank my God every time I remember you.

Stop Today and Taste and See that I am Good.

Taste and see that I am good. Survey the world around you, reflect on your relationships, your work, and your weekly encounters. Notice how I long to bless you, how I seek to pour out my goodness upon you and look for opportunities to shower you with my love. My kindness is at your doorstep, my peace meets you as you go to bed, and my grace wakes you up every morning. Just as you would stop and smell the roses, stop today, and taste and see that I am good.

_____

_____

_____

_____

_____

_____

_____

_____

Numbers 6:24-26

[24] *"The LORD bless you*
and keep you;
[25] *the LORD make his face shine on you*
and be gracious to you;
[26] *the LORD turn his face toward you*
and give you peace."

Enjoy the Rush for You'll Find Me There.

With the rush of the holidays and the end of a year, your mind can be in a million places. There's so much to do and so little time. There are preparations to be made and plans to set. The hustle and bustle is in full force and I don't want you to miss out on any of it. As you go from event to event, and task to task know that I delight in your goings, and in your pursuit to make sure everything is just right. I see all you do, all you prepare, and I smile upon you. Enjoy yourself in the rush; enjoy yourself in the going and take it all in knowing I am delighting in you.

_____

_____

_____

_____

_____

_____

_____

_____

_____

Romans 12:9-11

[9] *Love must be sincere. Hate what is evil; cling to what is good.*
[10] *Be devoted to one another in love. Honor one another above yourselves.* [11] *Never be lacking in zeal, but keep your spiritual fervor, serving the Lord.*

If You Seek Me You Will Find Me.

What a special day, a precious night - to know that even before time began, I was thinking of you, knowing the sacrifice my son would make so that you might live forever. I had you in mind then, and I have you in mind now. For the world I came then, and I will return for you once again. If you seek me you will find me, as you search for me with all of your heart, I will be there.

_____

_____

_____

_____

_____

_____

_____

_____

_____

_____

Luke 1:30-33

[30] But the angel said to her, "Do not be afraid, Mary;
you have found favor with God. [31] You will conceive and
give birth to a son, and you are to call him Jesus. [32] He will
be great and will be called the Son of the Most High.
The Lord God will give him the throne of his father David,
[33] and he will reign over Jacob's descendants forever;
his kingdom will never end."

388

Embrace this Life Today
& Every Day After!

This is a day where life is born, not only eternal life but also daily power and life. It's a time for celebration, a time to sit back in awe at the significance of this birth. Today life was born into the world – true life that surpasses our everyday worldly pleasures and touches on something deep down. The tragedy would be if you only embraced this life today and not the following 364 days of the year. His life is meant to affect yours each and every day. Of course, embrace it today, but wake up tomorrow remembering He's there for you once again.

_____

_____

_____

_____

_____

_____

_____

Matthew 1:20-21

[20] *But after he had considered this, an angel of the Lord appeared to him in a dream and said, "Joseph son of David, do not be afraid to take Mary home as your wife, because what is conceived in her is from the Holy Spirit.* [21] *She will give birth to a son, and you are to give him the name Jesus, because he will save his people from their sins."*

I am Waking You Up Today – Inside & Out, Outside & In.

I am awakening you today. No more comatose state of nothingness, no more dazing off into space, no more numbness around your soul. I am waking you up, inside and out, and outside and in. Like a cold bucket of water on your face I am giving you my life-changing joy today. This will sustain you through the dark and lonely times and give you the sustenance you need to keep going even when you feel so bogged down, when you feel the burdens of the day. I am waking you up today, inside and out and outside and in!

_____

_____

_____

_____

_____

_____

_____

_____

_____

_____

_____

_____

Matthew 1:23

23 *"The virgin will conceive and give birth to a son,
and they will call him Immanuel" (which means "God with us").*

My Voice is Your Map.

My voice is your map. Your very own roadmap, directing you, guiding you & leading you forward, onward in the way of my heart. One step in front of the other, my path is calling you. You've set your course & my voice will ensure you experience the desires of your heart. Keep listening, keep following and always know I am right here with you. My voice is your map – your guide for the future. Listen in today.

_____

_____

_____

_____

_____

_____

_____

_____

_____

James 1:16-18

16 Don't be deceived, my dear brothers and sisters.
17 Every good and perfect gift is from above, coming
down from the Father of the heavenly lights, who does
not change like shifting shadows. 18 He chose to give us birth
through the word of truth, that we might be a kind
of first fruits of all he created.

My Word Partnered with Your Voice.

When the enemy came at me, I responded, "It is written…It is written…It is written…" His word was hidden in my heart, ready to come to speak to me at the time when I needed it most. I experienced temptation just as you do. I understand the heaviness, the weight and the burden upon your shoulders as you try your hardest to run. In those times, use my tactics and speak aloud the truth as the enemy comes at you. Declare, "It is written…." as truth resounds from your lips. This is the weapon I've give you when temptation arises – *my word* partnered with *your voice*!

Matthew 4:4

*⁴ Jesus answered, "It is written: 'Man shall not live
on bread alone, but on every word that comes
from the mouth of God."*

No More Comparisons, You're an Original.

Today I proclaim that you are enough. Yes enough! No more striving to be perfect and no more seeking to surpass everyone around you. That's child's play. You know who you are - you're mine. You're created for victory, for opportunity, and for success. You are more than enough. Let my spirit remind you of this truth today, as you rest in my presence and relax in my gaze. You are enough I declare - more than enough. No more comparisons – you're an original.

_____

_____

_____

_____

_____

_____

_____

_____

_____

_____

_____

Luke 1:37

³⁷ For no word from God will ever fail."

One Shift and Everything Can Change!

Turn your eyes towards me - towards my beauty, towards my presence, and towards my voice. Physically, emotionally, spiritually, and mentally pivot your thoughts in my direction. One glance and I can give you a new perspective, one look and I can change your tone, one word and I awaken your senses. One shift and the game changes. Look for these opportunities today - to turn, to gaze, and to move towards me. One shift and everything can change!

Ruth 1:16

16 But Ruth replied, "Don't urge me to leave you or to turn back from you. Where you go I will go, and where you stay I will stay. Your people will be my people and your God my God.

Put Me as Your New Year's Resolution!

You have reflections on the year gone by and goals for the year ahead, but may I suggest mediating on you and me - our time, our connection, and our relationship. I see the months that have passed, and I see the ones that lie ahead, and I see all the desires burning in your heart. Let me help you achieve them; let me help you pursue them and let me help you make this the best year yet. It's in knowing me where you come alive, where your personality soars, insecurities vanish, and your confidence builds. Put Me on your new year's resolutions list and watch how so many pieces fall into place!

_____

_____

_____

_____

Song of Songs 8:6-7

⁶ Place me like a seal over your heart,
like a seal on your arm;
for love is as strong as death,
its jealousy unyielding as the grave.
It burns like blazing fire,
like a mighty flame.
⁷ Many waters cannot quench love;
rivers cannot sweep it away.
If one were to give
all the wealth of one's house for love,
it would be utterly scorned.

395

About the Designer

Briana Pettit, Graphic Designer

With a deep passion for art, Briana has a natural gift to turn a blank page into a colorful masterpiece. She loves to take an idea and create the perfect design you are looking for. Currently studying Graphic Design, she continues to add to her already advanced level of expertise. Briana lives in Myrtle Beach and has been married for 8 years to her husband Troy and has two kids, Caleb age 8, and Abbie age 3. She can be reached at bpettit3.30@gmail.com for more design opportunities.

About the Author

Mikaela Kate Schaefer

Mikaela Kate Schaefer is passionate to see you and your business reach its full potential. As a leadership coach she loves working with companies to see generations come together to increase communication and collaboration in order that they may achieve their best.

A speaker, writer, and coach, Mikaela Kate has invested 15+ years in developing men and women leaders from college-age and beyond. Her past experience in ministry, leading multiple teams, and engaging in one on one development makes her highly qualified to coach teams and individuals to help achieve their personal and professional goals. More recently she has worked with the manufacturing and retail industry, the financial and legal sector, start-up businesses, and with various independent sales teams.

A graduate of Iowa State University she discovered her unique gift for strategic thinking, people development, and investing in the growth of teams. After graduating she joined the college staff of Cornerstone Church in Ames, IA where she served as the College Coordinator. Later these skills equipped her to help plant Veritas Church in Iowa City, IA along with five other staff members.

From there she moved to Sheffield, England and worked as the Young Adult Director at St. Thomas Philadelphia. After returning to the United States, she became a Partner at DREAM Workplace to help companies grow their potential in each of their employees. Currently, she owns her own personal and professional coaching and training business (www.mikaelakate.com).

Mikaela lives in South Carolina where she enjoys time on the beach with a good book and spoiling her four nieces and a nephew every chance she gets!

She would love to connect with you and can be reached at releasingyourvoice@gmail.com

Made in the USA
Columbia, SC
16 August 2019